Nitinikiau Innusi

CONTEMPORARY STUDIES ON THE NORTH

ISSN 1928-1722

CHRIS TROTT, SERIES EDITOR

signature: Tshaukuesh Penashue

Nitinikiau Innusi

I Keep the Land Alive

Tshaukuesh Elizabeth Penashue
Edited by Elizabeth Yeoman

UNIVERSITY OF MANITOBA PRESS

Nitinikiau Innusi: I Keep the Land Alive
© Tshaukuesh Elizabeth Penashue 2019
Introduction © Elizabeth Yeoman 2019

23 22 21 20 19   1 2 3 4 5

University of Manitoba Press
Winnipeg, Manitoba, Canada
Treaty 1 Territory
uofmpress.ca

Cataloguing data available from Library and Archives Canada
Contemporary Studies of the North, ISSN 1828-1722; 7
ISBN 978-0-88755-840-5 (PAPER)
ISBN 978-0-88755-584-8 (PDF)
ISBN 978-0-88755-582-4 (EPUB)

Cover and interior: Vincent Design Inc.
Cover photo by Camille Fouillard

Printed in Canada

The University of Manitoba Press acknowledges the financial
support for its publication program provided by the Government of
Canada through the Canada Book Fund, the Canada Council
for the Arts, the Manitoba Department of Sport, Culture,
and Heritage, the Manitoba Arts Council, and
the Manitoba Book Publishing Tax Credit.

Funded by the Government of Canada | Canadä

Contents

Diaries of Tshaukuesh Elizabeth Penashue

Prologue

by Tshaukuesh Elizabeth Penashue

Before the protests, I couldn't have imagined I would ever be able to do all the things I've done. I have a recurring dream that I'm walking with other women across rotten ice in the spring breakup. We're in great danger but we keep walking. Sometimes in the dream people tell me I won't make it, but I always go on. In one version of the dream, my husband and I are driving a skidoo across a seemingly endless, narrow path of ice with open water on both sides. Then we come to a place where the ice path goes uphill and down again toward a rushing river. We turn at the bottom, and I ask him to let me down to see which way to go. Then we continue onward and we make it to the other side.

I've wanted to make my own book for so many years. I'm slow and it's hard work but I never gave up because this is very important. I want to see it before I die. It will be my legacy for my children, my grandchildren, my great-grandchildren, all my descendants. I know Elizabeth Yeoman helped me but it was still very hard work. I don't speak English well and I can't write in English but I explained everything to Elizabeth. When I was writing in Sheshatshiu or in nutshimit in the tent I had many interruptions and sometimes I didn't finish what I was writing, people needed me to help, children were hungry or they wanted me to play with them . . . so later Elizabeth and I worked together to complete the stories I didn't have time to finish earlier. Like my mother, I was so busy and so often interrupted. My mom had to keep the fire going, clean the caribou skins, make food. She took breaks but she always continued with her work. It's the same with my book. I'm an Innu woman like my mom, with many responsibilities and interruptions but I never gave up.

I first started writing when I went to the bombing range with my sister Rose Gregoire, Mani-Mae Osmond, and Jane the doctor,[1] and two men from Sheshatshiu—Tanien Ashini and Kanikuen Penashue. I didn't want to see the children lose our language, Innu-aimun, or our culture, and I could see that it was already happening. I hate to think that my journals could just lie there forgotten. I want people to remember this story. At first I started writing occasionally, just notes, but when I realized how strong the women were I wanted to write in more detail to tell our story. Until then we had never realized how strong we could be. Innu women never used to go out to meetings, but it was time to wake up and do something to stop the destruction caused by low-level flying and weapons testing.[2] We started the spring walk and the summer canoe trip to teach people about our land and about the Mishta-shipu, the hydro projects. When I first spoke publicly at Patshishetshuanau, a lot of people came to hear what I had to say. Later I was invited to speak in many places. I went to the bombing range with other activists. We put tents on the base to protest. We were jailed many times, in Goose Bay and Stephenville. We walked from Windsor to Ottawa and they put us in jail there too—Tshaki Ashini and me, Tanien Ashini and Penote Michel. I went to Europe twice to speak—Manian and Peter Penashue and their daughter, Thea, and Mani-Katinen Nuna and I went the first time. The Europeans put a flag supporting the Innu on Nelson's column in Trafalgar Square. The second time we went to Europe, Tshak and the Europeans put up a tent to show people what our lives were like and we held a walking protest. We went to court to support a Belgian who was in jail for protesting on behalf of the Innu. Back home, we walked on the Nutapinuant meshkanau on snowshoes to protest. Every day we walked and we had a lot of support— the Akaneshau brought us food, bread, and jam and other things to eat. We stopped at the Tshenuamiu-shipu and then we turned back. Once we walked to Manitu-utshu from the other side of the Mishta-shipu. We camped there for a few days. We walked to Minai-nipi with our children and four Innu from Uashat. Later we had to change our route to walk to Akami-uapishk[u]. Many young people have walked with me. I also organized canoe trips on the Mishta-shipu for over twenty years and many people joined us on those trips too. I try to educate my people, Innu people, especially the children, through these trips. We also do a walk on the road to Patshishetshuanau every fall.

Everything we do is to show the government that our culture and way of life are crucial for our survival. We can't go back to the old ways completely, but we must pass the knowledge and skills on to our children and grandchildren.

I began this work by studying and writing my journal. It felt so good to do that and it gave me strength. I want to help other women to be strong too. So many people have helped and supported me; they were so kind and welcoming; they respected me and they helped me get the word out. People from many backgrounds and places, in many parts of the world, and here in Labrador—when I'm at the bank or shopping, they come up to me to tell me they support my work. They give me courage to continue. Thank you to all of them.

When I started writing my book, I knew I didn't want a book with Akaneshau stories, just my stories. I don't mind if an Akaneshau helps me, but it's my book. When I started working on the book, I couldn't find anyone to help me but I kept looking. I asked one of my cousins, Germaine Andrew, who went to school in St. John's, my sister Nush, and Judy Pone—but none of them could do it. Germaine is very good at writing and reading, but she works in the clinic and she has her own children and grandchildren. I know she's too busy. But I'm glad I didn't give up. Another Innu woman in Quebec helped me for a couple of months, but it didn't work out. Finally, two women, Karlie King and Elizabeth Yeoman, came on my walk. They saw all the things I was doing and they wanted to help me.

When Elizabeth and I started to work together, we tried to find a quiet place to work and to eat our lunch. At Robin's house there was always something good to eat and somewhere to rest when we got tired. We always felt welcome there. She made hot food because she knew we didn't like cold dishes, and we would eat together with John, her husband, the judge.[3] He tried to speak Innu a little bit. He would pour my tea and say "nipishapui." Sometimes we told funny stories when we ate together. Everybody would laugh, and John would ask me to give him my plate so he could give me food. Now the book is finished and I'm very happy I didn't give up.

Introduction

by Elizabeth Yeoman

Walking with Tshaukuesh

Until I walked in nutshimit with Tshaukuesh, I could never have imagined how cozy it would be inside a tent in the wilderness at –30°C or how happy we would be: insulated by fir boughs and caribou skins, listening to the crackling of the fire in the rusty stove, breathing the scent of resin and wood smoke, illuminated by the flame of a single candle, the stories and laughter gradually subsiding as people drifted off to sleep; and then in the morning, waking up to the soft murmur of voices, the hiss of the kettle, the comforting smells of frying fish and bannock. Nor could I have known what it would be like to travel with a small band of people pulling all my belongings on a toboggan over frozen marshes and lakes, along forest trails and up into the mountains, under brilliant sunshine and through snowstorms; hunting and fishing for food, chopping chunks of ice from the river to melt for tea; the delicious warmth and comfort of it after a long day of walking on snowshoes. We had only each other to depend on, and though we did have a satellite phone for emergencies and occasional skidoos arrived carrying visitors, the outside world seemed very far away.

Tshaukuesh belongs to the last generation of Innu to grow up in nutshimit. She and other elders still know how to live there—how to stay warm, safe, and comfortable in one of the world's harshest climates. Tshaukuesh became an environmental and cultural activist in the 1980s and '90s during the NATO occupation of Innu land. Her outrage at the disruption of peaceful Innu life by the roar of supersonic fighter jets, at finding scorched trees and the remains of bombs on their land, at being told by soldiers that the Innu had no right to be there led to her becoming an eloquent leader of the

Innu tent in nutshimit. Photo: Jerry Kobalenko.

protests against low-level flying and weapons testing. Although Tshaukuesh had never before spoken publicly and her English was limited, she became a spokesperson for the Innu, imprisoned for peaceful resistance many times along with others. She testified at the Dutch Ministry of Defence and at the International Court of Justice in The Hague, and was an invited speaker at the John F. Kennedy School of Government at Harvard University, among many other national and international speaking engagements. Worried that she would forget important details, she began keeping a diary in Innu-aimun as a way of preparing herself for speeches, court appearances, and interviews with reporters. She had only been to school briefly, but her ability to write in her own language was the unlikely gift of an abusive teacher, a Catholic priest from Belgium. She seized the gift and made an opportunity out of devastating circumstances. The longer Tshaukuesh wrote, the more she knew she had to publish her diary as a book, a record of Innu history by an Innu woman who had lived through perhaps the most tumultuous and challenging times her people had ever known.

I first met Tshaukuesh when I interviewed her for a CBC Radio *Ideas* show about walking.[1] Marie Wadden, the producer, had documented the protests against NATO as a reporter and later in her book, *Nitassinan: The Innu Struggle to Reclaim Their Homeland*,[2] and she put us in touch with each other. I was in the studio in St. John's and Tshaukuesh was in Goose Bay with her daughter Kanani, there to help her speak in English. As Tshaukuesh described the annual weeks-long walk she leads on snowshoes through the boreal forest of Nitassinan and its meaning in relation to her quest for environmental justice and cultural survival for the Innu, she wept . . . and so did I. Somehow, across our vast cultural and linguistic difference and through our tears, we connected. The next year she invited me to join her on the walk, and so I did.

Not long after I returned home from the walk, a friend from Goose Bay called to say he was in St. John's and had something for me: a large cardboard box containing twenty thick school notebooks and a disorganized pile of papers covered with flowing handwriting in Innu-aimun. Although it was

At school in Sheshatshiu, around 1955. L–R: An Pone, Tshaukuesh, Shanut Rich, Matinen Ashini, Maniaten Ashini, Father Joseph Pirson, Shanet Ashini, Meki Atuan (Tipatapinukueu), Agnes Selma (Penipishkuess). Photo: *Them Days* archive, Happy Valley-Goose Bay.

Tshaukuesh writing in her tent, around the time she began her diary. Photo: Peter Sibbald.

often hard for her to find the time, Tshaukuesh had always had a strong sense of the importance of documenting what was happening. She also found keeping a diary therapeutic, and her writing evolved from brief notes into a detailed account of her own life and reflections on Innu land, culture, politics, and history. The contents of the diaries range from descriptions of daily life in nutshimit and in Sheshatshiu and details of the campaign against NATO—camping on the bombing range, encounters with the military, demonstrations and imprisonment; to her travels in other parts of Canada, the United States, and Europe as a spokesperson for the Innu; to lists such as one of all the women who went to prison with her and another of close relations who died; to jokes, recipes, and funny stories, information about medicine, birds, plants, and animals, letters to various people, and reflections on her ancestors and how they lived. She also recounts her fears and worries and writes short prayers. One of her most moving stories takes the form of a letter to her daughter, a senior administrator. She describes her conflicted feelings as her daughter leaves for work, elegantly dressed, getting into her car and driving away. For some this might be seen as the ultimate success, but for Tshaukuesh it is heartbreaking because "now you won't be able to go on the land." A letter to Premier Danny Williams reminds him that the queen has visited her tent and the least he could do is visit her too, so she can discuss a proposed hydro dam on the Mishta-shipu with him. Another letter, to a granddaughter, Pipun, on the day of her birth, laments the difficult world she has been born into and the overwhelming challenges facing the Innu.

My first reaction to the box of diaries and its implicit invitation was that the amount of work involved would consume the rest of my life, and that I was utterly unequipped to do it. I didn't speak Innu-aimun and I knew next to nothing about Innu culture and history. However, I soon realized that Tshaukuesh (and others who recognized the importance of the project) had been trying for at least ten years to get the diaries translated and edited. About one-third of the notebooks had been translated, some into English and some into French (which I do speak and read), but the translators who had worked on them were no longer available for various reasons.

A 2018 page from the diary, describing Tshaukuesh's sorrow that she was unable to complete her walk that year because she was injured in a skidoo accident on the first day of the walk. The small illustration shows her tears of disappointment. Photo: Peter Penashue.

2018
march 27

nin tstaukuen.
ute nitan skeslatkit
ume kaskikat miste mttheskikashu.
nimiste mitaten. kaue pipithian
eka menupit ushan nimiste
minuaten ume etutaman epijithian
nimiste ispititen niuatiniuen
espish ue tthispenotiman
innuse kie espish eka
pithiteni muian euie tnishkutor
muhau uaset tkeka utatau
kaishi iniut uihanishuau.
nete pet oia nikat. ispitentakeun
innu kaishi iniut eniuiak.
kie etepatkemustudau uaset
kie nusimiet ehun natim
etikau. nish 2 tkehuan miste
ispitentakeun etkishutemakuiek.
kie tkeka utaiek innu
kaishi iniuiak natim tkekthi
kunuetames. eukun uet
eka nita pitkitenimuian
ume etuta man. mithel tkehuan
nituten nipimishan nijupithin
nijumaten mesinat. nash
mithel jupun espish tietaman
tkekuan aju nieta pithitene
muian iat ianimaki natim
nitki eitin. eku nuthish
nustueten espit kaue pipithian.
nuskikuskin skitu. uenian
tthiesitstepaushit mettheskikat
niman tkthatatiman utthu kosmet
miste minuashiteh eittue ehun.

skash nithistan.
nitipatshiman. ehun nin tstaukuesh.

All of them were extraordinarily busy. The Innu are a small group. Only a handful of people have the skills to do this kind of work, and they are hugely in demand. They are the ones running the education system, writing the literature, the language resources, and the curriculum, as well as doing the myriad other tasks that require a high level of literacy in two languages and the cultural knowledge to be intermediaries between their own communities and outside governments and businesses. If the project was to be completed in Tshaukuesh's lifetime, somebody had to take it on, and she was asking me. I knew something about translation and about book publishing, and had published literary and journalistic writing as well as scholarly articles. As she put it, "You have your meshkanau and I have mine. Your meshkanau is books and mine is the land." It seemed impossible to say no after Tshaukuesh's extraordinary generosity and hospitality when I went on the walk. As I write this, eight years later, I realize that the project did consume my life but in a way I did not foresee: I have learned more from Tshaukuesh than I ever dreamed I could, and my life has been enriched in ways I never imagined. I hope this book will enrich many lives and adequately retell Tshaukuesh's extraordinary story in English.

The Innu

There are about 22,000 Innu. They are an Algonquian people and speak Innu-aimun, a language related to Cree. Although "Innu" sounds and looks similar to "Inuit," they are completely separate peoples who speak unrelated languages and have very different cultures. Innu territory includes twelve reserves and stretches across the eastern part of what the Canadian government and most maps call the Quebec-Labrador peninsula, from Mashteuiatsh in the southwest to Natuashish in the northeast and Pakua-shipu in the southeast. It borders on Inuit and Cree territories in the north and west and on the St. Lawrence River in the south and the sea in the east. About 2,200 Innu live in Labrador.

Tshaukuesh's diaries refer often to the Innu Nation and the local band councils. These are the official administrative organisms for the Labrador Innu, the Innu Nation being the overarching entity and each of the two communities, Natuashish and Sheshatshiu, having its own elected band council. However, the councils have little bearing on traditional egalitarian Innu decision-making processes. Colin Samson suggests that "any policy directed towards the Innu needed to elicit some level of *Innu* consent" (italics in original). He goes on to argue more broadly that Indigenous political organizations such as band councils were "manufactured" to protect the Canadian government from accusations of not recognizing the rights of Indigenous peoples.[3] The Innu Nation's website suggests more autonomy on the part of the Innu, stating "The Innu people of Labrador formally organized under the Naskapi Montagnais Innu Association (NMIA) in 1976 to better protect their rights, lands, and way of life against industrialization and other outside forces. The NMIA changed its name to the Innu Nation in 1990 and today functions as the governing body of the Labrador Innu."[4] Either way, the Innu Nation and band councils are clearly recent introductions. Several elected Innu leaders have expressed unease about their roles in these structures. During the Gathering Voices Inquiry, for example, Kiti, said, "As a leader you have to live on both sides, both the Innu and the non-Native way. You have to follow the white

Tshaukuesh Elizabeth Penashue and Elizabeth Yeoman. Photo: Robin McGrath.

man's way of living . . . It's really hard to choose which path you will go for the people."[5] Many others at the inquiry said that they were very concerned that the government only recognized the band council and Innu Nation leaders but not the Tshenut, the elders or traditional leaders and experts consulted by the people.[6] Tshaukuesh herself describes the situation like this: "Our life now is chaotic; long ago life was beautiful. There was no Innu Nation, no utshimau, no band council, we were our own utshimau. Everybody sat down together to make decisions and they made good decisions. We managed our own affairs, we were self sufficient: what to do about an accident or illness, where to hunt or camp, any issue that affected us we decided collectively."

Until the second half of the twentieth century, when Innu were gradually coerced by agents of the Catholic church and the provincial government to move to Sheshatshiu and Utshimassit, or Davis Inlet (and later from Utshimassit to Natuashish)[7] and to adopt the structures of the Innu Nation and band councils, most lived in nutshimit year-round, and the Quebec-Labrador border was meaningless. Because they lived on the land, they retained their language and culture, their skills and knowledge.

Inuit elder Sarah Anala remembers looking out from the residential school in North West River in 1959 at Sheshatshiu across the river: the pink sky of early morning and all the white tents scattered among the trees along the shore and up the hill. It gave her hope to see them there. And then one day the tents were gone and all the families were in their canoes paddling up the Mishta-shipu, the great river so central to Innu history and culture, to nutshimit. Somehow, although the Inuit children were in the residential school, the Innu were free then.[8] But their freedom and their ability to live in nutshimit were gradually eroded by others claiming ownership of the land (despite the fact that no treaties had ever been signed), by laws forbidding hunting and fishing, by pressure to put their children in school, by the destruction brought by dams, mines, and logging, by diseases they had not known in the past, and by the drugs and alcohol they turned to in despair. One of the greatest shocks in this long list was the construction of the hydroelectric dam at Patshishetshuanau in the 1970s and the flooding of more than 13,000 square kilometres of land, lakes, rivers, and islands to create the Smallwood Reservoir. Tshaukuesh recounts how the Innu were never consulted and only discovered the reservoir when they returned to the area as part of their yearly travels to find that all of the belongings they had left there—canoes, tents, equipment, everything they needed to survive—were under water, along with places where they had lived, hunted, prayed, and buried their dead. A further devastation came around the same time with NATO fighter pilots based in Goose Bay practising low-level flying over Innu land. In 1986 Canada signed a Multilateral Memorandum of Understanding (MMOU) with Great Britain, the United States, West Germany, and the Netherlands. As part of the agreement, as many as ninety-four low-level flights a day or up to 18,000 a year would be allowed. Since the area was perceived to be uninhabited because there were no permanent dwellings (a meaningless criterion in relation to a nomadic people), the pilots flew so low that at times they almost skimmed the treetops. The sonic boom created by the low-level flights was extremely stressful for the people and animals living there. The military also tested missiles over Innu land and tried to prevent the Innu from using the test areas.

And yet this tiny group of people, facing so many odds, stood up to the powers of NATO and the Canadian and Newfoundland governments to take control of their own land. Over the next few years, under the leadership of Tshaukuesh and others (many of them women), the Innu staged numerous protests, occupied the bombing range and the NATO base in Goose Bay, mobilized international support, and were jailed many times. Landmark rulings in the 1990s found them not guilty, establishing that they had the "colour of right" ("an honest belief on reasonable grounds" that they were right)[9] and that they "broke the letter of the law . . . to prevent a greater evil, that is, to prevent the destruction of the Innu people and their basic human rights."[10]

In 2010, following more years of protests and a negotiation process begun in the 1970s, the Innu Nation and band councils, the provincial government, and Nalcor Energy initialled the Bilateral NL-Innu Nation land claims agreement-in-principle, the Lower Churchill Project Impacts and Benefits Agreement (IBA), and the Upper Churchill Redress Agreement, collectively known as the Tshash Petapen, or New Dawn Agreements. The agreements have not yet been ratified by the Innu Nation, and the land claims document has not been finalized at the federal level.[11] The challenges the Innu face are enormous: the implementation of complex and controversial land claims

decisions; the further development of mines, forestry operations, and dams; the need to take control of their own education system; and dealing with all this via laws and a language that are still alien to most Innu. The Tshash Petapen stipulates that another dam will be built on the Mishta-shipu at Manitu-utshu (Muskrat Falls),[12] and that there will be well-paying jobs for Innu. The dam has been a key bargaining issue in the still-to-be-finalized land claims negotiations.

Tshaukuesh and her son Peter, vice-president of the Innu Nation in 2008 when they were interviewed by Shelagh Rogers on the CBC Radio program *Sounds Like Canada*, expressed different opinions about the dam at Manitu-utshu. Peter said that he did not necessarily want the dam but that it was going to happen anyway, and after their experiences with the first dam at Patshishetshuanau the Innu "have to have a place at the table." Tshaukuesh responded that "for a thousand thousand years Innu people hunted there." She described the beauty of the river and the land and warned of the poisoning of the water, fish, and animals that the dam would lead to.[13] Later she wrote in her diary about her conversation with a mining executive, expressing thoughts similar to those she had about the dam. She told him, "One day you'll finish working here and you'll go back to wherever you came from. You'll retire and you'll get a cheque every two weeks, and my people will still be here and our land will be destroyed." Though still not in operation, the Manitu-utshu dam has already destroyed land that was significant and important to the Innu. But as Tshaukuesh wrote, the Innu are and will still be there. Most Innu children still speak Innu-aimun, while only about one in six Indigenous people in Canada can converse in an Indigenous language.[14] Many Innu still

Innu canoeing on the Mishta-shipu. Photo: Jennifer and Kerry Saner-Harvey.

Tshaukuesh and family members with test missiles on the NATO bombing range. Front, L–R: Jimmy Nuna, Kaputshet, Patrick Penashue, Megan Rich, Paul Nuna, Pineshish, Jean Paul, Tony Penashue Jr. Back: Tshaukuesh and a man from Unamen-shipu. Photo: Kari Reynolds.

Fighter jet in nutshimit. Photo: Penashue family collection.

NEXT PAGE:
Protest in Ottawa. Jean-Pierre (Napess) Ashini, Celine Ashini, Ian Rich, Tshaukuesh, Manimat Andrew, Maurice Penashue, Tshaki Ashini, unidentified. Photo: Peter Sibbald.

Tshaukuesh and her husband, Francis Penashue, at Uinukupau. Tshaukuesh is holding a bunch of many different plants and flowers, and asking their spirits to protect them on the journey. Photo: Annette Luttermann.

Akami-uapishkᵘ. Photo: Jerry Kobalenko.

have prodigious skills for living on the land, while others have learned to live successfully between two worlds. The experience of their battle against NATO taught them that they did have power, even against such enormous forces. Their world has changed radically since Tshaukuesh was a child and even since she began writing her diary but, whatever happens in the future, Tshaukuesh's book is a remarkable account of Innu history during that extraordinary time of conflict, loss, and renewal.

About This Book

Diaries are not always orderly or complete. Tshaukuesh's diary is perhaps more than usually disjointed in the early years because of the circumstances of her life. There are long gaps between some entries, and often events are recounted briefly, with little context. One reason for this is that she did not have an established writing practice when she began. She was simply making brief, telegraphic notes for herself so she wouldn't forget things she wanted to say when interviewed in English. To compensate for this, we have added more recent writing about those times to some of the entries and editor's notes at the beginning of each section. Over time, Thaukuesh began writing in more detail, often as though she was confiding in a friend, and signing her entries "Nin Tshaukuesh" (literally "I am Tshaukuesh," but also used to conclude a letter, as in "Yours, Tshaukuesh").

In contrast to the brevity of some early entries, during periods when she was away from home and had a lot of time on her hands, Tshaukuesh wrote long reflective passages and nostalgic descriptions of life in nutshimit. Two significant times when this happened were when she was in prison, and during her stay at a treatment centre where she and her husband, Francis, overcame addictions, eventually becoming an inspiration to many others in the family and community to do the same. In later years, her sense of the importance of leaving a record growing stronger, Tshaukuesh changed focus again as she began to use the diary to document Innu history and culture. This final section (Part Four) is a lyrical and elegiac story of life in nutshimit. The last few entries in the diary have long gaps between them, perhaps because Tshaukuesh was dealing with the loss of fellow activists and loved ones, including her husband, and because she had so much responsibility for several of her grandchildren.

As the diary developed, Tshaukuesh also started collecting photographs that she and friends and family members took. When we began working together, we organized and scanned her photos and also approached professional photographers and journalists to license some of the beautiful and significant images they had produced over the years. Tshaukuesh points out that the pictures in the book are essential, both because many elders do not read written text in any language and because the photos will help people from outside the Innu world to understand the context better.

Another factor in the organization of this book is that Tshaukuesh had no community of writers when she began her diary. Most books by Innu are in French or English, and until recently Tshaukuesh read and wrote only in Innu-aimun. She wrote from her experience and from the Innu tradition of storytelling, as well as from her knowledge of jokes, prayers, lists, letters, and popular songs as possible narrative forms. She composed long sections when she had time, but many of her stories and notes were hurriedly scrawled in spare moments, sitting on an upturned bucket in her tent at dawn before anyone else was awake, waiting in a truck for someone doing their shopping in Goose Bay, travelling on a plane to a meeting. She invented or adapted the forms she needed as she went along.

Some of the early notebooks were originally translated by several people working directly from Tshaukuesh's original text and reproducing the meaning as closely as possible.[15] Their focus was on Innu literacy and language resources. At times they used a grid, placing matching sentences in Innu-aimun and English or French side by side. This sounds straightforward, but it really is not. Tshaukuesh often wrote hurriedly in point form, sometimes repeating herself and at other times leaving entries unfinished, intending to come back to them later but not always doing so. She often had more than one notebook at a time and wrote in whichever one she picked up first, so dates for some years are spread out over several notebooks and entries are not all in order. There are also many challenges in conveying Tshaukuesh's voice and the context she writes about in a language utterly unfamiliar to anglophone readers who don't necessarily know anything about her world.

The first time we sat down together to work on the book, Tshaukuesh handed me a note she had asked her brother to write in English. It read: "You don't have to write exactly what I said because my English is not that good. You can use other words but it has to mean exactly what I said." I did as she asked, listening to her oral translations and explanations of the written texts and correcting basic grammar and syntax as we went along. However, this is far from easy. Vanessa Andreotti, Cash Ahenakew, and Garrick Cooper point out that "scholars and educators working with indigenous ways of knowing are called to translate these into the dominant language, logic and technologies in ways that are intelligible and coherent (and, very often, acceptable or palatable) to readers and interpreters in the dominant culture."[16] How can a translation, in this context, "mean exactly what someone said"? Tshaukuesh herself recognizes this dilemma when she speaks publicly. For example, she often says the animals told her things and then follows these statements with "I know the animals don't really talk, but . . . ." She says she adds this disclaimer because her children told her the Akaneshau will think she's crazy if she says animals talk to her.

At first, I made audio recordings of our conversations but I soon realized that in the time it took us to be sure we understood each other, I could type what she said. I did a preliminary edit as we worked, discussing meaning and context with Tshaukuesh and, at times, with friends and family members if I couldn't understand what she meant. Most importantly, this process gave Tshaukuesh the chance to add and edit as she went along, to decide which parts were most significant, to take the time she did not always have in the hurried moments of writing the diaries. Much later we realized that the notebooks that had been translated by others had a very different quality from the remaining material: though these translations were more precise in conveying what was actually in the original diaries, they were not fleshed out and edited by Tshaukuesh in the same way and, despite the emphasis on transparency of translation, they reflected several different voices translating into two different European languages. Not only that, these early notebooks recorded some of the most historically significant moments of Innu history. To develop and edit them, we had to go back and work through them using the same process we had for the later notebooks. Tshaukuesh's daughter Kanani Davis, working with linguist Marguerite MacKenzie, is translating them back into standardized Innu-aimun for the Innu version of the book. The original handwritten diaries are in the archives of *Them Days* magazine in Happy Valley-Goose Bay, Labrador.

Of course, there are drawbacks to our collaborative translation process. The most significant one is our lack of a strong common language. Tshaukuesh's English, though eloquent and poetic, is limited, and my Innu-aimun infinitely more so—just adequate for a few basic needs and to make people laugh. And, of course, knowing a language well is also about understanding the culture. This is a serious problem, but, as Sophie McCall has written, "in every communicative act there is a gap—between teller and listener, between writer and reader, between signifier and signified. However, this gap can be a creative space in which new forms of agency and of voice may arise. . . . A diversity of forms of affiliation is possible and indeed necessary to recognize the struggle of writing and of telling a more just story of Indigenous presence in North America, through the mode of cross-cultural collaboration."[17] I do believe this, and it was the goal of our improvised process.

In this English version of the diaries, we use Innu names for places and some people (depending which name they prefer or are best known by) and Innu-aimun for some words that cannot easily be translated. The book includes a glossary, lists of people and places, and a map, as well as a timeline and a bibliography. The word "nutshimit," already used several times above, is just one example of a word and a concept that cannot readily be conveyed in English. It has been variously translated as "in the bush," "in the country," "on the land," "inland," and "in the wilderness." There is a similar range of possible translations in French. Recognizing the difficulty, Tshaukuesh often says in English "in-the-bush-in-the-country," as if it were all one word. It used to be that nutshimit was the opposite of uinipek[u], the sea, but now it has come to mean the opposite of the village or the reserve. Tshaukuesh often uses it this way, contrasting the health and happiness of nutshimit with the stressful disarray of life in Sheshatshiu. The late Innu leader Tanien (Daniel) Ashini was quoted as saying, "To reduce the meaning of the word 'nutshimit' to 'in the bush' does not describe what it means to us. It is a place where we are at home."[18] It is clear in the diaries that nutshimit also means home to Tshaukuesh and conveys a sense of continuity of a culture and a way of life.

In any good story or any meaningful piece of research, something is at stake. Nutshimit is what is at stake in this book: nutshimit; Nitassinan or Innusi[19]—the land of the Innu; and Innu-aitun—Innu life and understanding of the world. The book begins in the midst of the battle to save that world. Tshaukuesh's writing and the accompanying pictures give us a sense of what was at stake when the Innu stood up to the government and to NATO, and what is still at stake in the ongoing development of nutshimit. This book is both a story of the struggle to protect Nitassinan and a history of Nitassinan itself.

Walkers in nutshimit. Photo: Jerry Kobalenko.

NEXT PAGE:
Tshaukuesh's walks and other sites mentioned in the book. Artist/cartographer: Peter Jackson.

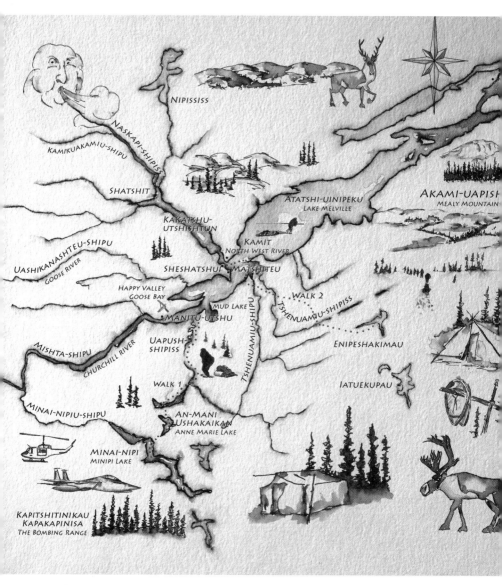

NIPISSISS

NASKAPI-SHIPIS

KAMIKUAKAMIU-SHIPU

SHATSHIT

KAKATSHU-
UTSHISHTUN

ATATSHI-UINIPEKU
Lake melville

AKAMI-UAPISH
MEALY MOUNTAIN

UASHIKANASHTEU-SHIPU
GOOSE RIVER

KAMIT
NORTH WEST RIVER

SHESHATSHUI • MATSHITEU

HAPPY VALLEY
GOOSE BAY

WALK 2

MUD LAKE

• MANITU-UTSHU

TSHENUAMIU-SHIPISS

UAPUSH-
SHIPISS

ENIPESHAKIMAU

MISHTA-SHIPU

CHURCHILL RIVER

TSHENUAMIU-SHIPU

WALK 1

IATUEKUPAU

MINAI-NIPIU-SHIPU

AN-MANI
USHAKAIKAN
ANNE MARIE LAKE

MINAI-NIPI
MINIPI LAKE

KAPITSHITINIKAU
KAPAKAPINISA
THE BOMBING RANGE

Atlantic
Ocean
NEWFOUNDLAND & LABRADOR
MAP
AREA
QUEBEC

Diaries of Tshaukuesh Elizabeth Penashue

Part One: 1987–1989

Editor's Note

The diary opens in March 1987 as many Innu families are in nutshimit at Akami-uapishk^u, hunting caribou. They know they will probably be charged with illegal hunting, but there is much more at stake. This is how they have always fed their families. The caribou is and has always been central to Innu culture and to their very survival. As Penote Michel, a leader of the resistance to the hunting laws, put it: "We are a hunting people. It is this form of living which lies at the core of our identity as a people, which gives expressiveness to our language, which animates our social relationships, and which for thousands of years breathed life into our people."[1]

RCMP officers have just arrived by helicopter to attempt to enforce the law. But change is in the air. Tshaukuesh's son Peter Penashue describes the events leading up to the opening scene of the diary: "We kept walking with our guns, leading the RCMP on a chase. We were afraid, we'd never done anything like that before, actually provoking arrest. In the past we would have hidden, but not anymore, we're through hiding. It's time our rights are recognized on this land. So, when those Mounties finally caught up with us, you know, I felt they looked at us with some respect because they could see we were doing what we thought was right, and they could see we weren't afraid of them anymore."[2]

Tshaukuesh herself also wrote later about what happened, described only minimally in the diary: "For many years we were not allowed to kill animals for food. . . . How did the government think the Innu would survive in the country if [we] couldn't kill animals for [our] livelihood? To me, this is the crime, what was done to the Innu. . . . The government told us we were endangering the herd, but in 1988, the very next year, they opened the herd

3

to a public hunt. . . . The white people always want to be the first to hunt in areas where the Innu have always hunted."[3]

Just one year earlier, Canada had signed the international memorandum of understanding that allowed NATO forces to test missiles and practise low-level flying of fighter jets over Innu land. The military exercises were not new, but this agreement allowed for a dramatic increase in the number of flights permitted. The Innu had never signed a treaty or formally ceded their territory, and for them, both the laws against hunting and the government agreements on military training were threats to their right to live peacefully on their own land. As the diary continues, we follow Tshaukuesh's story tracing the development of confidence and resistance strategies, and the arrests, court trials, and periods of imprisonment that ensued. The Innu moved from a local struggle to protect their hunting rights to the national and international spotlight as they took on what was then one of the most powerful organizations in the world, NATO.

1987

March 16

When the RCMP came in their helicopters we sat on the caribou our hunters had brought back so they couldn't take it—women, children, and elders. We screamed and stayed close together until they went away again. This showed us how strong we could be and we were very happy.

March 22

It's nine o'clock on Sunday evening. There was a big mass at church today. The priest blessed the oil and wine.[4] Our thoughts were with the people who are supposed to go to court tomorrow—they've decided they won't go. We'll support their decision and be strong.

March 23

Today was the last day of meetings for the chief and the lawyer.[5] Everyone spoke very well.

March 25

Today the Innu are waiting to be picked up by the police because they didn't appear in court. They'll probably be going to jail.

March 26

The people who went to jail yesterday are in court now—six Innu and the priest, seven of them altogether. We still don't know what's going to happen.

March 27

The seven people they arrested are appearing in court again now. They've been released from jail but they have to go to court again next month.

Caribou running. Photo: Peter Sibbald.

March 30

We're here at the caribou hunt near Tshenuamiu-shipiss. The chief arrived yesterday to stay for a while. He still doesn't know what the outcome of the trial will be. He'll probably come back here if he doesn't go to jail. This morning the men went out hunting, and we all hope they'll bring something back.

April 3

It's Friday evening. The women have been meeting to talk about our concerns. This July there'll be a band council election and Tanien is going to run for chief.[6] I hope these meetings and all our hard work to support him will help his campaign.[7]

November 8

We had a meeting about the school in Sheshatshiu, Peenamin MacKenzie. The people present were:

Me, Tshaukuesh
Rose Gregoire (Nush)
Judy Hill
My husband, Francis Penashue
Makkis Gregoire
Penute Antuan
Naomi Jack
Nuisha Pokue
Julianna Rich
Bart Jack Sr.
David Nuke

We don't have enough Innu teachers at the school. Ever since the school was built here in Sheshatshiu, our children are losing their history and culture. They don't live the way we used to and they have very unhealthy lives.

We should be allowed to run our own school; then we'd have a say in what our children are taught. The teachers have very different knowledge and beliefs than we do. The school doesn't have Innu books and the students aren't taught in their own language. What can we do for our children before it's too late? What will their lives be like if everything that matters is lost?

The water at the school hasn't been fit to drink for twenty years. We've spoken out about it but nobody listens. Neither the school principal nor the superintendent wants to hear about the concerns we have for our children's education. They tell us we have to look to the future, that all our knowledge of the land and the natural world, of nutshimit, isn't what the children need to learn.

The teachers don't understand that nutshimit is like a school where the children learn from their elders. When they come back from nutshimit, the teachers say they've failed and they have to repeat a grade, yet they learn so much there: how to find their way, how to use an axe and a gun, when it's safe to walk on ice, so many things. Innu-aitun and Innu pakasiun—Innu ways of doing things, independence and survival. The women teach the girls how to fish and get boughs for the tent and set snares. The men teach the boys to canoe and hunt. We have to teach them our culture—they need to know who they are.

Tshaukuesh and her sister Nush, a strong supporter of the women's meetings.
Photo: Peter Sibbald.

NEXT PAGES:
"They learn so much in nutshimit." Photos: Penashue family collection.

Pishum Rich putting wood in stove.

Manteu Iskueu Pone chopping wood.

Matthew Davis hunting.

Frederick Penashue brings home animals.

Tshaukuesh and child cutting fish at sunset. Photo: Jennifer and Kerry Saner-Harvey.

1988

February 17
The Problems We're Facing in Sheshatshiu
The leaders of Sheshatshiu—the innutshimau[8] and the pitutshimau[9]—don't bother to tell people what's happening and they don't have enough public meetings. We want to know where our money goes and how it's used. It's the chief's responsibility to tell the band council that our finances need to be managed better—for example, funding for the Outpost Program.[10] The band council should also make sure the garbage in the community is picked up regularly.

The poorest people in the community don't get the help they need. And some people are selling houses for profit when others can't find affordable places to live.

Why are some people treated better than others—the Akaneshau men who marry Innu women, for instance?

Even when the innutshimau aren't out of town for meetings, they're never in their offices. The only time we matter to them is when there's an election and they need our votes. Meanwhile, the councillors don't have the authority to approve anything until they talk to the chief. I think they should have some authority to make decisions.

There haven't been any meetings about our land since last fall. Our land is being used by the military to practise war, and no one seems to care anymore.

February 20
We hate seeing our leaders so focused on money. They're always asking the government for more. The government just wants us to be quiet and stay in one place. Pien Penashue[11] said that they want to control us, to keep us from hunting—that's why they give us pensions, so they can have our land. In the old days, nobody could tell us what to do. We were free.

March (undated)

In good weather, we cook outside over a fire—porcupine, beaver, caribou brought back by our hunters. Women hunt too, but we don't travel as far away from the tent as men do. Other times we check our fishing nets and clean the fish, then dry them over the fire. We pick berries, have a cup of tea, live peacefully. The children play nearby and we feel happy watching their fun. When we're all together like that, enjoying each other's company, I feel my heart opening up.

The fighter jets shatter our happiness—they have no respect. Sometimes they come in the morning, when the children and old people are still asleep in their tents. The little ones cry because they don't understand what that terrifying sound is, the sonic boom. It's so loud it hurts their ears, and we worry the damage might be permanent.[12] Sometimes we're out canoeing along the shore—hunting, fishing, or teaching our children and grandchildren our ways of doing things—and I'm afraid a canoe could capsize when people are startled. My grandson Jean Paul was playing on top of a big rock a long way from our camp when a jet flew over. He ran all the way home, shocked and exhausted by the time he got back. I told him not to go too far from the tent but he's too frightened to go out now anyway. That's what it's like these days in nutshimit. We never know when the jets will roar over our heads, so close to the ground—it's a constant threat. When I was a child there was nothing like that to fear. The Innu have been hunting in nutshimit for thousands of years and never experienced anything like this. Neither did the animals. It must terrify them too—they must try to get away from it but they can't. They need to be calm to eat and drink but they're always poised for flight. I wonder how it affects them when they're pregnant too—their babies are stressed just like ours.

March 25

Nin Tshaukuesh. I'm with Mani-Mae Osmond, Rose Gregoire, Francesca Snow, and An-Mani Andrew. The 20th was our first time in court. After the hearing, the priest and I were allowed to go home but Mani-Mae, Francesca, Rose, and Ani-Mani went back to jail. That same evening, I had a meeting in Sheshatshiu with Mani-Mat Hurley, Ellen Gabriel, Ann Hurley, and Janet Pone. We decided to put a tent up at the base again to support the women who are still in prison. The next day some of us did that, and they sent Paula

Andrew, Clem Andrew, Germaine Rich, Nuisha Penashue, and me back to jail again. I woke up the next morning and sat there in the cell with my hands on my knees. Everybody else was still asleep and I was thinking about what to say in court. I thought about my parents and all our ancestors for thousands of years. The Innu were always free—why are the women here in jail now? We didn't do anything wrong. We just tried to protect our land, our river, the animals, the children. This work is essential for our survival. I thought, "This morning when I go to court, I'm going to tell the judge that."

March 26
Tomorrow I'm going to court again.

September (undated)
Father Jim Roche, the priest, is at the bombing range fasting to support the Innu. He won't take anything except water. My son Matshen and Eric Andrew have tents set up there too, and so have Eric's parents, Maniaten and Sylvester. I heard that Jane the doctor is going to go and check on the priest, and Kanikuen Penashue and Tanien Ashini are going to go with her.

I talked to my sister Nush and Mani-Mae Osmond to see if they wanted to go too. I really want to go but I don't want to go by myself. Kanikuen and Tanien work for the Innu Nation and Jane is going to check on the priest, but I would just be an observer so I wanted company. They seemed open to it so I said, "Okay, I'm going to get ready. I'll see you at the airport early in the morning."

Undated
I didn't sleep very well. I was afraid Nush and Mani-Mae were going to change their minds. I prayed before I went to bed: "Please God, help me, don't let them change their minds!"

I got up early and put things in my backpack—my coat, my radio, tea bags and bread, milk, sugar, and a teapot. And I just got ready to go and headed to the airport. I was so relieved when I saw Nush and Mani-Mae there!

German F-4 Phantom reconnaissance training jet flying low over nutshimit. Photo: Peter Sibbald.

Innu children playing on a military target/simulated tank. Photo: Kari Reynolds. L–R: Kaputshet, Jean Paul, Katinen Nuna's grandson, Tony Penashue Jr. (standing), and Jimmy Nuna.

When the pilot found out we were going to come, he put a map on the table and showed us how far we'd have to walk. He said, "I'm only allowed to take the two men and the doctor inside the bombing range because they have work to do." He made me even more nervous than I already was but then Mani-Mae and Nush said, "That's okay, we're still going to go." I was afraid they'd change their minds when he said we'd have to walk, but they didn't. I was still worried about them though. My sister smokes too much and Mani-Mae has diabetes so she needs special food.

We walked and walked—it took us almost all day and there were swarms of flies. Finally, we got to a low hill where there had been a forest fire and the trees hadn't grown back yet, so we could see a long way. I could see a tent in the distance, and then I saw a military helicopter close to the tent. Maybe the military decided to send their own doctor and they wanted to get there before our doctor arrived.

Nush and Mani-Mae speak good English so they can talk to the Akaneshau. When they saw the helicopter, Mani-Mae said, "This makes me so angry! If I catch that helicopter pilot I'm going to say, 'Why did I have to walk here from so far away when you could just fly in? What gave you the right? It's our land, you have no right to be here!'" I was thinking, "This is great, you're going to be such a strong woman!" We kept walking but by the time we got there the helicopter had already left so Mani-Mae didn't get a chance to tell the pilot what she thought.

Maniaten had made bread and cooked a goose for us. I told her about our long walk and how tired and hungry we were. The priest was very happy when he saw us. He was emaciated—very very skinny. Maniaten said, "Let's go outside to eat so he doesn't have to watch us." We spread the tablecloth out on the ground and got ready to eat but then the priest came out, leaning on a stick. He said, "Go ahead and eat—don't worry about me—I just want to be here with you." It was very hard to eat with him there watching us.

We decided to wait until morning to walk around the bombing range and see what was going on. We were so tired we went straight to bed.

The next morning, we went to have a look. There were fuel drums all around the shore and the bombs had left huge craters in the ground, longer than an adult person and deep enough to stand up in. It's a wasteland. It

Scorched earth and fuel drum on the bombing range. Photo: Peter Sibbald.

Tent with cross and snowshoes. Photo: Camille Fouillard.

looks as though a giant bulldozer dug it all up. All the trees and plants are dead. There's nothing left for the animals to eat. It broke my heart. I'm sure my sister and Mani-Mae and I were all thinking the same thing: This used to be such a beautiful place. There must be a lot of animals around—black bear, beaver. . . . How do they feel? The beaver lives in the water, and the fuel drums are all around the lake.

Then we went back to the tent and talked about what to do. I said, "I don't trust them anymore. The government told us there would only be little test bombs, not real bombs. But they're huge." We have to tell everybody what the military has done. We have to do something to stop it!

In the evening, the helicopter came back. And although the pilot had told us he couldn't fly us into the bombing range, this time he did come inside to get us. I don't know why. On the way back to Goose Bay, we talked about having a meeting to tell people what we'd seen. I started worrying whether anybody would come, but we have to try. I kept thinking, "Please people, come!"

When we got back we went straight to Sheshatshiu and started inviting people to come. We didn't have time for much preparation and we only had a small office for a meeting room. When we got there I was so happy, I almost cried: people were streaming in, so many people!

We explained what we'd seen, the fuel drums, the bombs, the craters and the scorched earth, how they burned everything. Everybody agreed to have a protest the next morning. I was still worried though and I kept thinking, "Please don't change your minds!" I was so worried I could hardly eat.

The next morning, I got up and dressed warmly. When we got to Goose Bay, there were a lot of people, a huge crowd of women, men, and children. Nush and Mani-Mae and I were so relieved. We put up a tent on the base, working hard to get it up quickly and light the stove so it would be harder for the military to take down again. By the next day there were a lot more tents there and still more people coming.

October (undated)

A fighter jet was preparing to take off but it had to turn around because of us. I felt my heart open. We were so excited, we all applauded when we saw the plane turn back. We were very determined, all of us. I had never known how strong women could be until then. Until then I thought it was up to the men

to stand up to these forces, but since I spoke out, stood up to NATO, I will never again believe that there are any limits to what women can do. I even think they can be braver than men. Once we'd done it, we had the courage to do it again and again.

Undated

The military don't understand what they're doing to us. They're destroying everything we have—our land, our rivers, our animals, our happiness. Don't they care? So many people are crying in their hearts. We can never relax.

Low-level flying sign near the base in Goose Bay in English, French, Innu-aimun, and Inuktitut. Photo: Elizabeth Yeoman.

Tshaukuesh plucking a goose. Penashue family collection.

I have to get up early every day so I'll be alert and ready to comfort the children if the jets fly over. We just want to live in peace and look after our children. Everything we need and have needed for thousands of years is here in nutshimit and now they're taking it away from us.

They just point at the map—with one wave of a hand they decide where to go. To them it's an empty space. They don't care about the people hunting here, teaching their children how to live, or about the animals. They have no idea what this means to us or even whether anybody is here at all.

November (undated)

I think the military must have had a meeting to decide what to do about us. We were starting to think they wouldn't show up this time, but then around six in the evening the RCMP arrived with the base commander. They were acting a bit crazy and they cut the lines on our tents, so we were pretty scared. All our food and everything was out in the tents because we'd been making supper, so we rushed to put everything away. The RCMP told us to get out and be quick about it, so I tried to rush to get my little grandson dressed and he burned his arm on the stovepipe. They didn't arrest me, probably because he was crying so much.

Some people went to jail, and some went home. But as soon as we had a chance to talk to each other again, we said, "Let's come back tomorrow morning with more people and put up more tents." We did that, and I guess when the military saw how many of us there were, they decided to leave us alone because they didn't come back.

December (undated)

We've been here for about a month and a lot of Akaneshau have come out to support us. One evening when Betty Peterson[13] was staying with us, I invited the women to get together for a meeting in my tent. We lit candles and made everything nice. Some other Akaneshau came too and John Olthuis,

An evening in the tent with peace activist Betty Peterson, lawyer John Olthuis, and other guests. Back row, L–R: Rafael Gregoire, Ben Andrew, unidentified, unidentified, Tanien Ashini. Front row, L–R: Dennis MacKay, Betty Peterson, unidentified, unidentified.
Photo: Peter Sibbald.

Lawyer John Olthuis with elders Mishen Pasteen and Mani Pasteen.
Photo: Camille Fouillard.

the lawyer, was there. I asked why they never invite Innu women to their meetings. Only the men have travelled, they've gone everywhere—Ottawa, Toronto, Halifax, England—just the men. Why not the women? They didn't answer, but I think they thought about it and maybe they realized I was right.[14]

We had more meetings and the women had a lot of good ideas. And then my answer came. At that first meeting, nobody answered when I asked why only the men were invited to meetings. But not long after that, I was invited to speak at Uapush. The military were holding a meeting there and the women were invited. That was my answer.

At the meeting, there was a long table with glasses and water on it. The military were at the table, and the Innu sat at the end of the room. We talked about the land and the animals, respect for the environment. This was the first time in my life that I spoke in public, the first time they invited me.

Tshaukuesh speaking, Shishin Rich to her left. Photo: Camille Fouillard.

1989

April 19

We were protesting at the base—women, men, and children—and the soldiers came with a pile of riot sticks in the back of a truck. One of them picked up a stick—I think he wanted to hit us—but another one told him to put it back. We were scared but still determined to stop the low-level flying. We all worked together and each of us tried to set an example of courage for the others, even the little children. We knew the risk but we also knew we had to do it.

I was arrested, and I asked the RCMP to let me say something to all the people gathered outside. I asked for somebody to translate into English for me but nobody volunteered; I guess they were afraid. I heard my sister call out, "Can somebody help Tshaukuesh?" but still nobody came forward, so I just spoke in Innu-aimun. I said, "We have to do this. We can't give up! We were invisible to the government until we started to protest but now they have to pay attention."

April 20

We're in a tiny cell. Why are we in jail when all we did was try to protect our land? It's not a crime. Somebody passed some papers through a flap in the door. Women from all over had written to us to tell us that they supported us, they were thinking of us, praying for us, they knew how hard it was for us, how all of us had children and grandchildren we had to leave behind, how worried we must be about them, how they must miss us. It strengthened our morale enormously to get those letters. I'll never forget it.

At ten in the morning the RCMP told us we had to go to court, and at the hearing another woman and I were told we could go home but the rest of the women went back to jail. I still don't know why. As soon as I got home I started organizing another protest.

April 25

I was arrested again, and when I walked into the jail I heard all the other women clapping. We're in and out of jail all the time now and every time we get out we organize another protest to support the people who are still there. It's very hard, though. One morning when I was leaving for a protest I was in tears, I felt I couldn't go on. My youngest son, Pineshish, and my little grandson Kaputshet were clinging to me and crying, "Don't go, Grandma!" "Don't go, Mom!!" "Don't worry, I'll be back," I said. "Don't cry." But it was very very hard to walk out that door and to be strong through all of it. I keep reminding myself that I'm doing this for all of us, for everybody. I didn't want the children to see me crying so I held back my tears until I was going down the steps.

April 26

At the bail hearing I talked about my parents, who lived free on their land. We are no more guilty of any crime than they were. We didn't hurt anything or anybody. I talked about how I want to be strong for my children. Most people were too shy to speak, so whenever I spoke everybody was whispering to me what they wanted me to say. It was very confusing with them all telling me different things to say.

I'll never forget what happened next. The judge said, "There will be many Elizabeth Penashues." I didn't understand, so I asked the other women what it meant afterward and they said maybe he meant that there will be more strong women fighting to protect their land and organizing others to do the same.[15] I think this judge understands us somewhat, understands what we're trying to do, because he's an Inuk.

NEXT PAGE:
Tshaukuesh hugging Kiti (Katie) Rich, with unidentified Mountie in background. Photo: Penashue family collection.

Innu women outside the courthouse. Back left: An-Pinamen Pokue, Tshaukuesh. Front row, L–R: Nush (Rose) Gregoire, Julianna Pasteen Hill, Tshanet Pone, Tshaki Ashini. Photo: Penashue family collection.

Tshaukuesh sitting in entrance to tent. Photo: Penashue family collection.

Part Two: 1990–1997

Editor's Note

There are no diary entries for 1990, but the photos by photojournalist Peter Sibbald document a three-month, 850-kilometre walk from Windsor to Ottawa to raise awareness of low-level flying in Nitassinan. The same distance could be covered by a fighter jet in a single hour. Walkers from Sheshatshiu included Tshaki Ashini, Jean-Pierre (Napess) Ashini, Raphael Gregoire, Selina Ashini, Manimat Hurley, Tanien Ashini, Penote Michel, and Tshaukuesh. There were also many Indigenous and Akenashau walkers from other places. Penote Michel, Tanien Ashini, and Tshaukuesh were arrested with others for blocking the entrance to the Department of National Defence Headquarters in Ottawa during a Remembrance Day protest.

Tshaukuesh remembers the walk as poorly organized and difficult. Perhaps it was an omen of things to come. Although protests continued and there was still national and international support for the Innu, results were not always positive. Some leaders were beginning to feel that negotiations with the provincial and federal governments were a more realistic way forward. Christopher Alcantara describes the negotiations as slow because of "persisting and increasing internal distress (i.e., alcoholism, drug abuse, Third World living conditions), all of which were highlighted by suddenly interested media."[1] Leadership changed frequently, and much of the energy and expertise within the community went to addressing these issues, along with "struggling with the federal and provincial governments over policing, the judicial system, relocation [of the Mushuau Innu from Utshimassit] to Natuashish, logging, mining and other economic development activities."[2] In 1996, a framework agreement, a key step in the negotiations between the

Innu and the provincial government,[3] was signed by Tshaukuesh's son Peter, then president of the Innu Nation, and then Premier of Newfoundland and Labrador Brian Tobin.

Meanwhile, Tshaukuesh continued her campaign to protect the environment and Innu culture. At the beginning of 1991, she and others were protesting against logging on their land and awaiting a visit from Premier Clyde Wells. A forestry report written later describes the area that was being logged as "a unique ecological landscape" and expresses concerns about the impact of "road developments, past timber harvesting activities, and human-caused forest fires . . . changing water levels and flow patterns resulting from the Upper Churchill hydroelectric development." The area is also characterized as one of "the world's [last] remaining large intact natural forest ecosystems— undisturbed industrially and large enough to maintain all of [its] biodiversity."[4]

In 1993, a huge nickel deposit was discovered at Emish, or Voisey's Bay, on land claimed by both Inuit and Innu, and the two groups often met to discuss strategy on this front. There were also protests during this period about hydro dams and provision of electricity, ranging from Labrador Innu refusing to pay for hydro power that came from the first dam on the Mishta- shipu, for which they had never been compensated, to demonstrations against proposed new dam constructions in Quebec and Labrador.

By the mid-1990s, there was renewed international interest in the Innu, especially in Europe, because of a 1996 NATO-Canada memorandum of understanding to expand military training activities in Labrador. The new agreement would allow 15,000 test flights a year, an average of over forty flights per day. The environment was also a key issue in the ongoing struggle against NATO occupation. The federal government had implemented an environmental assessment prior to proposed expansion of the NATO base. However, as Tanien Ashini saw it, "The problem there was that the government controlled the process, and was being manipulated with interference by the Department of National Defence. To complicate matters, the project was scaled down from a full NATO base, when NATO decided they didn't need a base, to military low-level flight training only. We found the assessment to be biased in favour of the Department of National Defence. We eventually boycotted the environmental assessment because of this and other reasons."[5] The panel ruled that there was not enough scientific evidence to support the Innu arguments that the flights were harmful.[6]

Following two weeks in jail in September 1993, described by Tshaukuesh in her diary, Peter Penashue made the connection between militarization, the threatened environment, and the cost of government oppression of the Innu:

It becomes a travesty when you consider the fact that the Newfoundland government will be spending more than $50,000 to lock us up, not to mention the thousands of dollars that they have already spent prosecuting us for our "crimes," all in the interest of "justice." This is while we suffer the impacts of militarization, and while Canada and Newfoundland reap the benefits. It is pure hypocrisy for European countries to export their flights to Innu land when they don't allow them at home. We care about our land as much as they care about theirs, but somehow we don't seem to count.[7]

The Royal Commission on Aboriginal Peoples was established in 1991. Their final report describes this period as

a time of anger and upheaval. The country's leaders were arguing about the place of Aboriginal people in the constitution. First Nations were blockading roads and rail lines in Ontario and British Columbia. Innu families were encamped in protest of military installations in Labrador. A year earlier, armed conflict between Aboriginal and non-Aboriginal forces at Kanesatake (Oka) had tarnished Canada's reputation abroad—and in the minds of many citizens.[8]

However, the authors went on to describe the period also as one of hope, a time in which Indigenous peoples were rebuilding connections and communities. This was the context in which Tshaukuesh and Francis began healing their own relationship and family and community connections in 1992, through completing an addictions treatment program in Windsor, Ontario. Throughout the '90s, Tshaukuesh also continued to participate in protests and speaking tours related to logging, mining, and hydro dams, as well as protesting the NATO occupation and the environmental assessment, occasionally expressing concern that the Innu were not as united as they had previously been in these struggles but never giving up or compromising on the goal of protecting the land for future generations.

Perhaps another reflection of the turmoil of this period is the fact that diary entries for the years 1993–5 were mixed up and many were not clearly dated. We did our best to sort them out, but Tshaukuesh couldn't always remember and we weren't always able to confirm dates in other ways since some of the original diary entries either do not include much detail or they document events that occur every year. Therefore, while the events themselves all took place, the dates for entries during this period may not always be accurate.

1991

July 8

My husband and I are on our way to St. John's. I'm really nervous because I'm afraid of flying. He's sleeping as I write this. I'm so frightened, the only thing I can do is pray. I cling to my rosary and my Bible. Faith is powerful and no matter how afraid I am, I know the Creator is with me.

I often feel alone and afraid. I always find it so hard to get on a plane, but it's important for us to continue our fight against the government. If we don't, I believe they'll just keep developing our land until they destroy it completely. We have to protect our children and our people.

I often thank the Creator that the Innu have woken up and found strength in each other to walk this long, hard road together. We are all very strong.

Nin Tshaukuesh

Penote Michel in front of the Parliament Buildings in Ottawa, 1990. Photo: Peter Sibbald.

On the bus to jail, 1990. Photo: Peter Sibbald.

At Manotick, Ontario, during the walk to Ottawa: "We covered our faces to avoid breathing the fumes from passing trucks on the highway." Photo: Peter Sibbald.

Arrest of Tshaukuesh at the Department of National Defence, 1990. Photo: Peter Sibbald.

September 5

We're here protesting at Shatshit Meshkanau, blocking the road because we want to stop the logging. Enough is enough. We will not have our trees cut down in our home. Our land is still very beautiful and the Innu use it wisely. It's our children's inheritance, their future.

September 24

We're camping here because a government representative is coming to talk about the logging. We set our tent up first and then we pitched the big tent, which has ten panels. It's huge. We picked spruce boughs and spread them over the tent floor. At first there was just me, Tshaukuesh, and my sister An Pinamin. Then George and David Nuna came with two children. I can't believe we did it. I think the Creator must have helped us, because everything went so well. We cooked caribou meat so all the Innu people and the government representatives could eat together. We barely had enough time to cook but in the end, everyone had plenty to eat.

October 1

This is the best month because everyone seems healthier. I can feel it in my body: people are getting strong, coming to life again.

November 1

Today was a beautiful day. We're just back from checking our rabbit snares by the North West River road. Even our food tasted better because I was feeling so happy. I have so much work to do, but I haven't started it because I wanted to write this in my diary first. I know where this happiness comes from. The Creator has taken pity on me because he has seen tears in my eyes so many times.

November 5

We've forgotten many things that are important about our land because we're so wrapped up in other things. We've had so many problems since the election. I wish we, the women, could get together sometime.

Newfoundland and Labrador Premier Clyde Wells at talks about logging. Photo: Peter Sibbald.

December 18

This morning I woke up from a scary dream. I was very upset and got up to check the time. It was seven thirty and already bright outside. I felt better once I realized morning was coming. I dreamt that three of my children were missing. We thought they might have drowned, but then we found them. When I saw them, I grabbed Kanani and I was so happy.[9] I think the Creator is trying to tell me that whatever I lose in life, I'll always find it again, and I shouldn't be afraid.

December 19

Today we went to Nishuasht Kaitashtet on the North West River road. We took seven school students with us. The weather was very nice but a little chilly. After we cooked and had something to eat, I got dressed and went to pick boughs for the tent floor with one of the teachers. I was walking in front of her when I spotted pineu tracks leading to where the bird had taken flight. I looked up to the top of a tree and there it was, a pineu. Wow! Deep in my heart, I was very happy. I thought that the Creator was showing us this bird. We killed it and cooked it for supper. We all had such a nice day.

Tshaukuesh serves caribou to the premier and land claims negotiators. L–R: Clyde Wells, Ray Hawco, unidentified, Tshishennish Pasteen. Photo: Peter Sibbald.

Winter camp. Photo: Navarana Igloliorte.

Akami-uapishkᵘ. Photo: Navarana Igloliorte.

1992

January 4

Yesterday my husband, Francis, and I came to Tshenuamiu-shipiss. It was a lovely day and not cold at all when we left. When we got to Matshiteu, Tuminik and An Pinamin were waiting for us. Tuminic was cutting down small trees to mark a path across the ice. We drove off on our skidoos toward the river and stopped at the end of the path to set up camp. The next morning, the weather was perfect, and Francis and Tuminic went hunting for kak^u. An Pinamin and I went for a walk. We saw pineu twice during our walk but we didn't have a rifle. When we got to the top of the mountain, we looked all around us and it was very beautiful.

January 9

Our work is going well—we're cutting fresh boughs for the tent floor and throwing out the old ones. The tent is very cozy and the children are having a lot of fun. In the evening, I went for a walk over the frozen marshes and I enjoyed it so much that I didn't want to turn back. When I finally did turn around I was facing a mountain, and it reminded me of a time when I was a little girl in nutshimit with my parents, when we were camping near a mountain that looked a bit like this one. We'd had a successful caribou hunt and there was plenty to eat for all of us—a good memory.

It's really nice in nutshimit. Whenever I think about the past, when life was going well and we lived here all the time, I miss it terribly. Every day was a good day and the Innu were strong and healthy. Today the government has made us very poor. Why did they have to find us when we had such a good life on our land?

January 30
We're back in Sheshatshiu. I did something today that made me feel very brave. I drove the skidoo all by myself, towing our food and belongings in a komatik.[10] It was a long way, and it's the first time I've ever driven a skidoo that far. I realized that I can be strong when I want to be.

February 6
We're very poor in Sheshatshiu, but if we work hard and look after each other we'll do better. One thing we can do is to help the young people. They're losing our Innu way of life. I wish they could be taken out to nutshimit this spring. They'd enjoy it so much and they'd be much healthier. They spend so much time in school, but it's not doing them much good. If we don't teach them now, they'll be helpless in the future.

February 15
Last night something terrible happened in Utshimassit. A house burned down and six children who were left alone there died. The parents were out drinking. This is a huge tragedy. Alcohol is killing us more than ever. We've lost our way of life.[11]

February 27
Our priest left Sheshatshiu, our long-time priest.

This morning I had a hard time getting up. I didn't feel like eating, but I forced myself. By nine o'clock, my children were at school and the others had gone to work. After everyone left, I started to cry. I was afraid someone would come through the door and wonder why I was crying by myself, so I went to my room and started praying to Saint Anne and then I felt a bit better. It's very difficult when a long-time friend leaves. We've been friends for so many years with Father Jim. How could he just leave us like this? People don't know why he left so suddenly. He has deeply hurt the people who cared so much about him.

March 12

This evening I'm flying to Toronto. I'm terrified of flying, so I'm praying on the plane. Three of us are travelling together: Mani-Katinen Nuna, my son Matshen, and myself. This is hard work, a lot of travel, but we want to see the children in a better place while we're still living. We'll be landing soon. I hope everything goes well with the conference. We're here to talk about our land.[12]

March 27

We're at a friend's house in Toronto. He has three boys, no girls. This man is very nice to Innu people. He says we can stay at his house anytime if we don't have a place to stay. So far, we're doing okay out here. Hopefully our conference will be worth all this hard work. We really miss our children and wonder how they're doing since we left. I find it very hard to call them and when I do I feel even lonelier, so it takes me a while to call.

March 30

Here we are in Peterborough. We're really tired. Mani-Katinen, Matshen, and I spoke at the meeting. It went well, except for one thing: we don't speak enough English. There are some things we weren't able to say though we tried really hard.

In the evening, we had a communal supper in this nice house. There must have been thirty people. The Akaneshau were shocked by the way the Innu are treated on their own land. Some of them had never heard about this, but they took our words seriously and seemed to appreciate what we had to say. I tried hard to explain clearly so they could understand.

April 2

We're still in Ontario, back in Guelph. The woman whose place we're staying at is really nice; she has two children—both of them look as though they're Uinipaunnu.

We finished our presentation at the school. This evening we're speaking again to a large gathering. We're so tired but we believe we're helping a lot of people by travelling around like this to tell our story and explain what's happening to the Innu.

Skidoo. Photo: Melissa Tremblett.

37

April 7

We got back to Sheshatshiu yesterday. One time while we were away I called my husband and he said: "It hasn't been nice here since you left." I told him: "It's always nice here. The sun shines every day." I think the good weather is an omen that we'll be successful in our struggle to keep and defend our land. We want a beautiful earth. Is it possible that my thoughts will become reality?

Nin Tshaukuesh

April 19

Today I came to nutshimit with three kids: Pineshish, my last born, and Kaputshet and Megan, two of my grandchildren. When I boarded the Twin Otter in Goose Bay, I was very anxious, and then during the flight the wind picked up and we couldn't see anything. The children were throwing up and I was really frightened. Then suddenly it started to clear, the sun came out, and I was so relieved. Finally, we landed and pitched our tent.

I realized too late that I'd brought too many grandchildren with me. I didn't factor in how much work they would create for me, along with all the other work of living in nutshimit. I was just so happy to be coming. But I've ended up regretting it because I just don't have enough time for my grandchildren with all that I have to do.

Still, it's a joy to be here and the children seem so healthy; they're always smiling. They love it here and that makes me happy.

April 20

This morning it snowed a lot but it cleared up in the afternoon. After putting Megan to bed, I chopped firewood and then I went to look for spruce boughs.

April 21

It's lovely out today and the children are happy. We killed some caribou during the winter, and now the men are going to retrieve the meat.

April 23

This morning I set up my tent—it took me all day. First I cut the poles, and then I dragged them into position. I sharpened the ends to a point. I managed that much but I haven't been able to go look for boughs for the floor yet.

I've been thinking a lot about my older children and how I would have liked them to be here to help me. In truth, not one of them wanted to come with me to nutshimit. Me, who has so many children.

April 24

Today the weather's really nice. Tuminik, Tashtu, Tanien, and his girlfriend went off somewhere. I'm really envious of them, and on top of that it's really nice out. I felt sorry for my son. He really wanted to go with them, so I asked Tanien to take him and in the end he did.

April 28

We're feeling great today. It was the first time we've eaten kak^u in a long time and it was very fat. This evening I was a bit sad, though. We didn't have any firewood, so I asked Pineshish to go and chop some. He went off with one of his friends and they brought back some logs and sawed them up. He reminds me of Matshen when he was young, always trying to help no matter how hard it was. That's what I was thinking, how so much has changed now.

May 4

My husband arrived today with other family members so we put up another tent, but when we were done it seemed too small to hold everybody so we took it down again. I started working at lengthening it and we managed to get it back up by evening, and then we transferred our belongings.

May 6

Today Tashtu and I went to look for spruce boughs. It's really nice out. The men have gone fishing and won't be back until evening. I imagine they're having a good time.

It's scary to hear the fighter jets here. They fly so low, startling the old people, and we're frightened too. It's totally unacceptable for them to fly over nutshimit.

May 7

I'm disappointed because this evening there'll be a float plane coming and my children want to leave. I feel so sad that they're leaving because I love having them here in nutshimit. My daughter says she's sick, so finally I agreed for her to go. I tried to keep my grandson but she didn't want to leave him. I'm so disappointed that they're going back to Sheshatshiu.

May 8

Today my sons and their father have gone hunting with the other men. I'll work at home and look after my grandchildren.

May 9

We got up this morning to a very damp day. It was snowing but we did our work anyway. My husband, son, grandson, and I went to get spruce boughs, which was hard because there wasn't any crust on the snow at all to walk on, but in the end we got them and then we started moving our campsite. We were in the middle of taking down our tent when the plane arrived with a priest and my sister Nush on board.

After the visit, we finished taking down the tent. If you could only know how much I enjoyed this day. It went so well, thanks to my children's and husband's efforts, as well as my own. We all worked together to move our campsite and that made me so happy.[13]

May 10

The weather was perfect this morning, so we decided to go for a boil-up.[14] We took all five children and they had a lot of fun. We couldn't decide where to make the fire because it was so beautiful everywhere, but finally we made it on a bare patch in the snow. I felt so happy watching the children sliding and then all of us eating together around the fire.

May 11

Today I made a call on the shortwave radio and spoke to Maniaten, who told me some news: "The Innu from Ekuanitshu and Uashat have organized a march." It's very exciting. One of my sons, Matshen, is participating in the march, and they're supposed to walk all the way to Montreal.[15]

Tshaukuesh taking a break in the woods. The uishuaushkumuk (yellow moss, lower left in photo) is good to insulate one's feet in winter. Photo: Kari Reynolds.

"I set up my tent. It took me all day." Photo: Lucas Meilach-Boston.

Tshaukuesh with children. L–R: Megan Rich, Pishum Rich, Petshish Jack. Photo: Peter Sibbald.

May 12
We slept in late and really enjoyed our afternoon. We went skidooing: me, my son, and Tashtu, to a place where Tashtu had camped before. The ground was already bare because the snow had melted there and the site was really beautiful. On the way back, we picked berries that were still there from last year.

When we were getting ready to leave on the skidoos we heard a sudden loud noise that frightened us, so we ducked down. It was the fighter jets.

May 13
Today isn't a good day at all, rainy and foggy. We can't see anything. We had to move our campsite in the pouring rain.

May 14
Today we went to look for spruce boughs with two of the children. The weather still wasn't very nice, but we got them and made a floor in the tent. We weren't able to do it yesterday so we had to sleep on wet sand, very uncomfortable.

May 15
The men went off to hunt geese and ducks and to fish. They'll be back this evening. They took the boys with them: Pipitsheu, Pineshish, and Kanapash.

May 17
It was really nice out this Sunday morning, so we went on a skidoo to look for spruce boughs. We spotted white pineu, and since my husband was away hunting I went ahead on foot to see if I could get them. I was in the mood for a good walk and it was so beautiful there. I didn't sink into the snow at all because it was frozen hard on top. While I was walking I thought about my mother and father, who also loved being in nutshimit. Once their children were grown up, they always hunted together. They never stopped working except to sleep, but although their work was endless, their happiness was too. I often think of them when I'm working and also when I'm really looking at

Tshaukuesh and children in tent. Photo: Kari Reynolds.

Nikashantiss Penashue. Photo: Kari Reynolds.

the earth, like when the ground starts to emerge from the melting snow in spring. When I walk and look around me, I think to myself that they'd enjoy this so much. Thinking about all this makes me miss them.

May 18

Kanani, it's me, your mother, writing you. Today the weather is very gloomy, not nice out at all. It's raining, the kind of weather I hate when I'm in nutshimit. Early this morning, it was nice for a little while. Now I'm not feeling very well. I wanted to tell you that Pipitsheu is really tiring me out because he always wants to go back. I know what he's trying to do. When I scold him, he says: "I should go home because I'm in the way." I've given it some serious thought, and I think I'll send him home when the plane arrives. I haven't told him this. I talk to him gently. Could you tell Tshak to talk to him too? I'm worried he might start drinking. Nachelle is helping me with this letter. I'd love Ishkueu to come back. I really thought she would. I'll come home early if your father leaves, because there won't be anyone to help me with the firewood and all the rest of the work. I'm really disappointed that you weren't able to come to nutshimit; you always helped me so much here on the land.

There's something else I wanted to say to you. I'd like you to wait a while before you give your child up for adoption. Don't give the baby away until we've seen it. It's a big decision. Your father hasn't said what he thinks yet, but maybe he'll tell you.

May 23

We're at Mishtutshashk^u at the head of the rapids. We can't go home—the weather is terrible. It's snowing and there's zero visibility. Yesterday we tried to get through on the road to Iatuekupau but we couldn't. The storm was raging when we set out. I didn't say anything but I couldn't help wondering what we'd do if I got sick. There was no way a plane could have come out, and even the skidoos would have been useless because the visibility was so bad. I was really frightened.

Nin Tshaukuesh

May 28, Inland at Iatuekapau

A lot of us are sick, including some of the children. It's cold and the sun rarely shines; there's rain and fog all the time. There are many Innu in nutshimit and I'm sure they're all thinking the same thing about the weather—things are going badly for us.

Nin Tshaukuesh

May 31

Tonight, we're in Montreal, but we have to go home to Sheshatshiu. Yesterday, the Innu who were on the march reached their destination after walking all the way from Uashat. It was so good to see them, and they looked very strong. I hope they'll always be that way. A lot of people were waiting to support them on their arrival. I walked toward my son and hugged him. I wanted to cry but I managed to control myself.

June 5

When I got back from Montreal, my sister Maniaten called me on the radio to invite me to her camp at Kapinien-nipi.[16] As soon as I arrived this afternoon we moved the campsite and then went to look for spruce boughs. We're all staying together in her tent. It's very pleasant but there's one thing I'm really sad about: Maniaten can't do anything because of her poor health. I know how she feels. She hates being idle all day, unable to move. I feel so sorry for her; she used to work so hard. Today her heart is sad.

June 6

This morning it was lovely out. We did chores in the morning and in the afternoon we went along the shore in a motorboat and then stopped to make a fire and eat a very good lunch.

June (undated)

We're in a plane heading back to Sheshatshiu already. It wasn't going very well at Kapinien-nipi because I'm so sad about my sister being sick. She's angry that she can't work or even walk.

June 25
Today we're at Patshishetshuanau on our way to Esker. We're waiting for the train to come, but it will still be quite a while before it arrives. This afternoon we went to see where the river has been lowered by the dam and we were taken to visit the inside of a rock mountain. We went down 800 feet below the surface and looked for a long time, feeling so sad to see our land destroyed like this.

July 12
I often think about the past. Sometimes I can't find anyone to confide in, or it takes me a long time to find someone. After sharing my troubles, I gather my thoughts in prayer or sometimes I cry. Two things really keep me going: the Creator's support, and my own efforts to pull through.

July 21
I'm thinking about all the times we've had huge problems. Once again, my children and I are in a bad situation because my husband has started drinking again. It was hard when the children were small, and now it's my grandchildren. What will become of us?

July 26
I want to write about what I did in Sainte-Anne de Beaupré.[17] In the morning when we got up, it was miserable rainy weather. I went off by myself to join a friend. We went to wash up together and then we ate and returned to our tent. Later on, I went out again to go to mass. I was so upset I cried. I couldn't stop thinking about my husband. I went to buy a few things and I bought more than I could afford, so now I'm completely broke. I didn't eat anything for lunch—I went back to the tent and lay down for a while to try to sleep. Then I went to pray.

I often feel sadness in the bottom of my heart because of my husband and my children, and I think about what my mother used to tell me: "Don't marry a man like that." But I didn't listen to her. After my marriage she said, "You can stay here in my house, you can take my bed," but my husband didn't want to, so we left with our belongings. My mother said, "It will never work out for you." This broke my heart. I hope never in my life to say such a thing to my children. It still hurts me a lot.

July 28

We arrived in Ekuanitshu from Sainte-Anne de Beaupré yesterday. This evening I went to visit Enen Munin and Shushtin, and we went to see a man named Papia. I couldn't help but feel sorry for him. He hasn't been able to walk or speak since he had an accident while he was drunk. When we went to see him the first time, he burst into tears. I pray for him and feel so badly for him.

July 31

This morning after breakfast I phoned the person in charge of the festivities.[18] I asked if I could sell doughnuts and he said okay, so I started making them right away. I was feeling sorry for myself and my children, and I know they felt sorry for me too. I truly didn't think my husband would start drinking again. I don't know why he fell off the wagon. I'm really upset and very disappointed. I feel so alone.

August 7, Uashat

It's a beautiful day today. Last night we went to the Mishta-shipu with a group of Innu men and women to heal ourselves in a sweat lodge. I really didn't think I'd make it to the end of the long ritual because it was so hot, but I managed to stay. It was one o'clock in the morning by the time it was over. Then Peter and I went home.

August 11

I want to say something I've been thinking about a lot. I can't help feeling overwhelmed, because I want to do everything possible to fulfill my children's needs. I'm heartbroken, especially when they ask me for money and I don't have any. Tonight, I bought some lottery tickets and I won $73. When they brought me the money, all my children ran to me. They were so excited and so was I. We're really pathetic but I have to be strong. I pray a lot.

September 14

Tonight I'm going to visit a nun. I've wanted to see her for a while, to talk to her about the great ache I have in my heart. I also want to ask her if I can pray at her place where it's quiet, or perhaps if we can pray together. That's what I want to ask her.

September 28

This afternoon I went to the Innu community health clinic because I was sick. There was a sled outside with a dog attached to it, and when I went to pass him he bit my leg. Nush was getting out of the car and I yelled out to her: "The dog bit me." She came over to see, and I went into the clinic where they took care of me. They gave me a shot and some medication. I wonder why that happened to me. I've had such problems lately that I was already close to despair, and being bitten by that dog just makes everything seem worse.

September 29

It's really nice out today. After lunch, my children and grandchildren and I went for a walk along the road. I was very happy when we got to our camp. We went to check our snares, but we hadn't caught any rabbits. It's really nice to be in the woods, though, and the path we took to the snares was so pretty.

October 12

Today some Innu from Sheshatshiu entered the military base through the fence. The soldiers said, "No, you can't go in." But they're lying; it's not their land. It's the Innu people's land and we will keep it. There were fifteen Innu and their children. The military police handcuffed some young people and grabbed others by the arm.[19]

October 16

Today I'm leaving for Montreal to speak at a conference with my son Tshak and an Akaneshau. I hope everything goes well and nothing happens to us. We're going to discuss how much the land has been damaged and the ongoing destruction. I'm still afraid of flying but I just keep praying. Tshak is sleeping, even though he's probably as scared of flying as I am. We'll be arriving soon—we're landing now. That's all. I hope everything goes well for us at the meeting.

Nin Tshaukuesh

Hauling toboggans in nutshimit. Photo: Penashue family collection.

A boil-up in nutshimit. Photo of pots and pans on fire: Penashue family collection.

Tshaukuesh and Francis on their wedding day. Photo: Penashue family collection.

October 19
This morning we're in Bennington, Vermont. We've already been to two cities.

October 20
We're in a school and have already spoken to two classes. I'm trying to defend my cause by speaking out about it. This is hard work and we're getting really tired.

October 22
Dartmouth College (New Hampshire): We gave a talk in a school again. Then tonight we gave another talk in a church. It took everything out of us. We were exhausted from all the talking. We never rest.

October 24
We're arriving in Montreal from the United States. The Akaneshau who brought us couldn't find his way to the airport; we were on the road a long time and it was pouring rain. I was really scared.

November 1
This afternoon we wanted to go pick berries but we couldn't because it was snowing so hard. Tonight, I can't help feeling a lot of sadness in my heart because I'm living through so many things and they aren't just little problems, they're all big ones. I have to go away again to join my husband at the treatment centre. If he hadn't started drinking, we would never have had to go through this.

November 8
I'm in St. John's. We landed at one-thirty and will board another plane at two. I haven't stopped crying since leaving Goose Bay. I know I'm going to a place where I can get counselling, but I find this very hard. Then I tell myself: "There is a God." I just need to trust in him; he's the one who'll watch over my children while I'm away. He'll watch over me too, because he is very powerful as well as merciful. I'm all alone on this trip and I don't understand English, but I remind myself that I'm not the only one in this situation. Sometimes I still feel angry, though, when I think about how strong a dependence on alcohol can be and how it changes the behaviour of men, how it controls

them. It's merciless. I detest it. Alcohol destroys us—our bodies, our children, our culture. If alcohol didn't exist, we would never have experienced such poverty here on earth.

November 10

I'm going to force myself to do everything in my power here at Brentwood.[20] I find this really hard because I have so many children and grandchildren and I worry about them all the time. I arrived here on Monday and the next day after lunch, I was taken into a room where I would have classes. I didn't feel comfortable at all and I was really scared. There were lots of women and I didn't know anyone. When the time came to go drink coffee, the Akaneshau were talking really loudly, and some of the women looked strange because of all their makeup. And they smoked a lot. Tobacco makes me sick. I was thinking, "I'm going to be sick. How will I manage to stay here?" I was hardly able to pour my coffee, I was trembling so much. I wanted to leave, but there was no one to go outside with me and I couldn't tell what the weather was like. At least I managed to say what I had to say in English. Since I've been here, I can see that I am being helped and that I am finding solutions. I never used to understand what "you're not alone" meant, but now I know it means: "You're not the only one to experience this. There are many others who are living through the same thing." This is the first time I've understood this.

I don't know anyone here, and I don't have any friends. I ask myself, "Why did I come on this trip?" I'm afraid of not being able to see my husband and then when I do see him, they don't let us talk and we're not supposed to look at each other. In the afternoon, they put us all together— the men and the women. I saw my husband arrive, but he didn't look at me at all. I ask myself: "What will happen to me? What is happening to me?"

November 12

I've been at Brentwood for a few days. I still find this very hard, but I got permission to see my husband and now I'm feeling a bit happier. I was able to tell him what I needed to say, and as I was leaving I asked him to pray for me. I want to do everything possible to help myself. I pray constantly. I brought holy water with me and holy oil from Sainte-Anne

and I use them all the time. Sometimes I talk to the Creator and ask him to give me health, even though I have a lot of problems. I'll be grateful if he grants my prayers.

Sometimes I ask myself what I came here for anyway, since I don't touch beer anymore, but I know I have a lot of anger in my heart and I need help. However, I don't understand why we have to go so far away to get help and why we had to leave our children. I wonder why we can't get help near Sheshatshiu.

November 14

Something amazing happened this morning. We all met, lots of people, men and women together. Those who had finished their three months each took turns speaking at the microphone. Then it was this woman's turn to speak. I know her; she has always helped me and she's very nice. She was almost crying while she spoke. All of a sudden, I heard her say my name and realized she was talking about me. When I heard all that she was saying, I didn't know what to do. I was surprised that she even remembered me.

The Akaneshau were watching me cry. I was thinking that the Creator wanted to show me something, that he wanted me to hear with my own ears something that would make me very happy because he has seen the distress I had in my heart. When this woman finished speaking, she sat down. Afterward when the men got up, they all went over to congratulate the people who spoke. I went over to see the woman. I was still crying. I hugged and kissed her and told her: "Thank you very much, you made me so happy. You really helped me." I'm still amazed by what happened. I was always looking for someone to help me but I didn't have anyone to confide in. I'm always afraid people will tell others what I tell them in confidence.

I always live with frustrations, but they only last for a short while. Bit by bit I find solutions. Now that I'm here, I'm finding help with my problems. My heart is opening because I've had someone to talk to. The anger I have in my heart will lighten.

Nin Tshaukuesh

Children protesting at the base in August 1993. Photo: Kari Reynolds.

Women protesting at the base. L–R: Manimat Hurley, Lyla Andrew, Nastash Qupee, unidentified, Tshaukuesh, unidentified. Photo: Bob Bartel.

Innu protesters in front of a Dutch F-16 fighter jet, August 1993. Photo: Kari Reynolds.

Tshaukuesh writing with bandaged hand. Photo: Penashue family collection.

November 17

Last night I woke up after midnight and couldn't fall back to sleep. I tried everything. First I prayed, then I turned on the lights and reread my diary. Finally I fell back to sleep, and I dreamed I was in a canoe with my son, my son-in-law, and one of my grandsons. I was yelling at them, but my son and son-in-law didn't seem to be paying any attention. Suddenly I saw my grandson drifting, and I was going in the same direction. My son-in-law caught him and then I grabbed on to him. He was soaked so I took off his clothes. I was very upset but at the same time relieved that we'd rescued him. Then I woke up and it was almost seven o'clock, so I got up. I feel that the dream was a good omen. Even if I live in difficult circumstances, everything will be all right. That's how I interpret my dream.

November 19

A short while ago a woman came in and she seemed to be really sick. She sat down and started to cry. I felt a lot of compassion for her and I understood the depths of her sadness. When I looked at her, it was like looking at my own reflection.

November 23

Since I've been here, I'm beginning to understand more and more things I wasn't aware of before. I've learned that we can't look too far into the future. We have to take one day at a time.

November 27

My son arrived last night. We went to meet him at the airport. When I saw him, I was so happy, but this morning when I got up I immediately thought about how he was going to be leaving again already. I hated to see him go. I thought about him while we were at the airport, about all the times I had to run away with him when he was little so his father wouldn't mistreat him. Now he's an adult and he has very important responsibilities with his work. He's a very strong person now.

This is the last stage of the program, if we finish it, of course. Sometimes it's very hard; it's as if I were in prison. You have to be strong.

Tshaukuesh's grandson Manteu Pone, snowshoeing. Photo: Jerry Kobalenko.

December 3

This morning the women and the priest got together to talk. I've been wanting to speak for a long time, so when it was my turn to say something I asked a question. I was trembling and my heart was pounding. I was tongue-tied and afraid I'd be sick, I wanted to die, but then suddenly my fear disappeared. I could feel the Creator helping me. I said, "This isn't my language, maybe you won't understand me, but I'm doing my best." I felt so much better afterward, because I'd managed to say what I wanted to. I've done all I can to see this through, no matter how hard it is.

Nin Tshaukuesh

December 5

If only I can remember all that I've come to understand and what I've learned from Father Paul: not to worry about others so much, to look after myself but without putting pressure on myself, and not to force myself to tell my husband what's wrong but instead do what will make me happy, to make changes a little bit at a time and not rush things. I shouldn't expect that everything will go well for me right away; I have to be patient and work at it. That's just how it is.

Nin Tshaukuesh at Brentwood

December 6

Today we returned from Brentwood to Sheshatshiu. I couldn't wait to be home again. When I got off the plane several of my children were there—I took all of them in my arms. I felt as though I was coming to life again, I was so happy. I looked at them there at the airport and I said to myself: "I have a lot of responsibility." I thank the Creator. I thought so much about my children and my grandchildren that it hurt.

December 14

It's nice out today, not cold at all. I hope we'll go fishing.

December 25

Christmas morning. When I got up I hadn't slept enough and I was really tired, but I had a lot to do. We talked about eating together, but I decided to get started with my work first. Once the house was warm, the children got up and opened their gifts. While they were tearing off the wrapping paper, I suddenly started to panic. I thought I wouldn't have time to do everything I wanted to do, so I told them to go to church. I had only gone the night before, and now I thought it was their turn. I wanted back to work but my hands really hurt—they're all cracked from working outdoors so much. What could I do? I started to wash the dishes first, to soak my hands in the water. After the dishes I made the bread, and then I started cooking. When they got back from church one of my daughters came into the kitchen and said: "I'm going to make a pie." I was really happy. I wasn't expecting her to help me. Then she started to make the pie without asking me to show her how to do it. I said to her: "This afternoon, you should go over to where they're distributing presents. Take the children, you can finish the pie later on." But they were gone for a long time, and in the end my other daughter made the pie with a bit of help from me, a delicious partridgeberry pie. We had just enough time to prepare a good supper and then we all ate together. I'm so grateful to the Creator. I never thought it would all work out, because I was so tired and my hands hurt. They still hurt as I write this—that's why my writing is so bad.

1993

Letter to an Akaneshau woman (undated)

Munik,

How are you? I'm okay. Today I received the little cars you sent. My son and grandson love them. As I write this, they've shut themselves up in a bedroom to play with them. I wish you could see how happy they are. Thank you so much, you sent them really quickly.

I still haven't gone to nutshimit, but I've almost finished doing the things I need to do first. I'll thank the Creator if nothing happens to us before we go. Keep praying for me, okay? Every time I see you I'm very happy. I think of you as a friend. When I go away, I really miss my land, my children, and my friends, but when I see you I feel better. I know it's because of your kind heart that you're helping the Innu. If you could come with me to nutshimit, you'd see that we're happy there, that we work hard and that the children are happy. When we had that last meeting with the Akaneshau who support the Innu, new people attended, and I told them what I thought: "It's difficult for you to really know the Innu people."

That's all.

March 21

We've been here at Tshenuamiu-shipiss since Friday night. It's so good to be here.

I've been thinking about the old days. When my mother didn't go hunting with my father, she went on her own in the area near the camp. She set snares, she hunted pineu and kak^u, she fished. While she was busy with that, we older children took care of the younger ones, which we really enjoyed. We also helped with the tent: the boys cut down trees for poles, and the girls got boughs for the floor and cooked.

I loved learning from my parents when we were in nutshimit. We were never impatient or dissatisfied. We were always happy and we always slept well.

March 23

Three years have gone by since we defended our land. We endured a lot of hardship. The women were arrested, the men and children too. We broke through the runway fence many times at the site where our land is occupied. We joined forces to get inside, and we helped one another.

April 5

I've been very unhappy since we got back to Sheshatshiu. I wish I could go back to nutshimit. I love it there so much and we're so healthy when we're in the bush. I'm sorry we left.

September 8

We're in jail here, six children and twenty-one adults. This place is not acceptable. We're so thirsty. The children are very unhappy.[21]

September 23

When we were united in our efforts to defend Nitassinan, the women were very strong and they had a lot of support. They aren't speaking out so much now, and the international media has lost interest. It makes me so sad. I've worked so hard and suffered so much to try to help my Innu brothers and sisters, the young people, my children and grandchildren. I wish we could see some progress, evidence that at least some gains have been made here in our homeland. The government has destroyed so much of our land, and there are many more things they will do to destroy the Innu. My heart is broken.

Nin Tshaukuesh

October 5

We've arrived in Quebec and are now on the bus on our way to Ottawa, still a long way from our destination, with three more hours of driving. When we get there, we have a lot to do. We're here to show the government how we feel about the way it's treating us, how it has destroyed so much of our Innu way of life, and how so much has been stolen from us.[22]

Nin Tshaukuesh

The women

Mani-Katinen Nuna
Ishkueu Penashue
Tshaukuesh Penashue
Nuisha Penashue
An-Mani Andrew
Penitenimi Jack
Shanimesh (Germaine)
Kanikuen
An-Makanet Nuke
Naomi Jack
Kanani Penashue
Akat Piwas
Manishan Nui
Tenesh Rich
Kiti Rich

The children

Nuisha's daughter
Mani-Katinen's granddaughter
An-Mani's daughter

Pineshish (Robert) Penashue
Nikashantess

The men

Utshesh Nuna
Peter Penashue
Kanikuen Andrew
Atuan Penashue
Tanien Ashini
Matshen (Bart) Penashue
Penote Michel
Makan Jack
Kanikuen Penashue
Shapetesh Abraham
Shuash Gregoire
Tshak Penashue
Hak Penashue
Shuashim Nui
Makan Jack
Atuan Nuna
Apenam Pone
Tshenish

November 5

Today the chiefs left for St. John's. They want to find a way to force the government to stop their hydroelectric projects on the rivers. They're also going to tell the government what we'll do with the electricity, so we don't have to pay for it. They'll be back tonight. It was really good to see them on television this afternoon.[23]

November 23

I've been really upset, night and day. All of a sudden, the phone rang. It was Manishan calling from Uashat. We're very good friends and we talked for a long time. I feel from the bottom of my heart that she really helped me.

On the Mishta-shipu. Photo: Annette Luttermann.

Sunset on the Mishta-shipu. Photo: Jennifer and Kerry Saner-Harvey.

1994

May 4

We left this morning to break trail and set up the tent at the place where the military launches missiles: my husband and me, Atuan Penashue, an Innu man from Pakua-shipu, and two Akaneshau. There were quite a few of us, including children. The snow was wet and heavy and we were pulling the children on sleds, so we were very tired. Night was falling when we arrived, so we set up camp and organized things outside. We were almost done when we heard a skidoo. It was the military approaching the camp. They stopped nearby, on the edge of a small river. They couldn't get across so they yelled out, "You can't camp there! You're trespassing." We yelled back to them in Innu-aimun, "This is our land. It's Innu land." Finally they left, and we helped people who were still setting up their tents and looked after the children.

Nin Tshaukuesh

May 9

Today we had nothing to eat. All of sudden, someone called out that caribou had been sighted. We left to look for them on the skidoo and managed to shoot one of them. We were very happy, looking forward to eating meat for the first time in a long time, but when I looked more closely, it didn't look good, it didn't seem to have any blood. It also tasted funny, so we couldn't eat very much. I thought right away that it's because of the fighter jets that the animals are like this.[24]

Nin Tshaukuesh

"We couldn't take our skidoos because we were afraid the military would confiscate them. And the helicopter pilot wouldn't take us. So we had to walk." Walking into the bombing range. Photo: Kari Reynolds.

May 15

Our companions have left for Minai-nipi, where they'll camp while we stay here. We have two tents, ours and one that belongs to an Innu from Unamen-shipu. We're here with our children. I'm upset at being left behind by the others in the group. It didn't work out because there was too much conflict and jealousy, and we couldn't work together. The tent seems so empty and I'm feeling very hurt. I feel that I don't have any real friends and there's no one I can talk to, to share all the sorrow I have in my heart.

Nin Tshaukuesh

May 18

It's a beautiful day here in nutshimit. After lunch, we left—me and my grandson, Peter's son. We walked along the river to hunt pineu. After a while we stopped to rest and talk where the snow had melted and the ground was bare. I told him what was happening with us, the Innu at Minai-nipi. He listened very carefully. Before talking to him I was feeling very upset, but after I told him what we're doing, I felt happier. He's still young, only nine, but even when he's grown up I'll still tell him stories. When he's older I'll remind him:

"We walked along the riverbank in nutshimit and we sat down on bare ground where the snow had melted, and I talked to you. There was no one else there, just you and me."

May 29

Sunday—the weather was a bit gloomy and changeable. Once in a while the sky cleared a bit, but we weren't sure if it was going to be nice enough to do anything. Finally the sun came out in the afternoon so we left, my husband and I and a couple from Unamen-shipu, to have a picnic in a beautiful place. I really love this life.

Kaputshet, Jean Paul, and Pineshish holding signs reading "Property of Land and Resources, Danger, Target Shooting Area, If There Is Target Shooting Do Not Enter," and "Property of Land and Resources, No Trespassing, Federal Land and Resources, Government." Photo: Kari Reynolds.

Innu flag flying as Tshaukuesh walks outside her tent on the bombing range. They knew the military were just behind the hill and, anticipating confrontation, had not slept well. Photo: Kari Reynolds.

June 1
Today is Wednesday and we're still in nutshimit. We called Sheshatshiu and were delighted to hear that my granddaughter was born this morning. I thank the Creator for such a beautiful gift.

June 4
We're still here in nutshimit. We came to protest on the bombing range, but we failed because of not being able to get along with each other. It's sad, because there were so many things we could have done. If the ice had melted, the children would have loved to go fishing and we could have taken them canoeing and hunting: for ducks, beavers, all kinds of animals. On Sunday, we could have gone for a boil-up and had a picnic together. As it was, as soon as I arrived I realized things weren't going to go well, but I still did my best to organize the protest to put an end to the testing of missiles in our homeland where we hunt.[25] This is Innu land. Sometimes I feel so frustrated and have so much pain in my heart that I cry.

Nin Tshaukuesh

June 15
We're about to take off. This will be the last flight before we get to where my son Tshak is taking courses at the university. I'll be so happy to see him. I often wish I could see him when things aren't going well and tell myself that if he was here with us, he'd help us. That's what I think.

June 16
I'm very far from home, in Edmonton, thinking about my son Pineshish. Today is his birthday and he's thirteen. When I was leaving I said to him, "Pineshish, we'll bake you a birthday cake when I get back home."

June 20
Tshak, I'm so happy to see you all graduating at the end of your studies. And I loved your speech. You were thinking about the children, and they're very important to me too.

July 22

We're on the train to Uashat and I want to carry on to Sainte-Anne de Beaupré, because prayer has helped me many times. My husband has already left to drive back home on his own. I'm thinking about him and I feel sorry he has to drive so far. He helped us by bringing us here, and now I think he must be very tired.

Every time I'm on this train, I look out the window at the route my parents walked, year after year. The Innu have travelled across this land for thousands of years. When I look at the vast territory they traversed, I think about the hardships they endured and how resilient they were. And they didn't even think it was hard. For them, their way of life was their well-being and their strength. They weren't under pressure but they never stopped working, except when they were sick. They never had to pay their children to help them.

August 13

Ishkueu's daughter was born today. She's doing well, and so is the baby. We're all very happy. I'm so grateful that she decided to keep the baby. Of course, she'll be tired—she'll have to raise her daughter and take care of all her needs. They wanted to put the baby up for adoption, but I was absolutely opposed to that. I did have sympathy because it will be hard, but I was also very upset.

August 19

At Innu Nikamu.[26] They're playing a traditional Innu ball game, like the Innu used to play a long time ago, and kuaskuetshikaunanu, nipitekateshimunanu, and utshipitunanu pishanapi, as well as Akaneshau games. The canoe race for both men and women is at one o'clock, and there's also a relay race in which they wear funny costumes and each participant has to put the costume on at the beginning of their turn, run to the other end of the racecourse, then take it off again for the next person to put on. Then there's emikuan mak napatat, atikunanu, and kashustatunanu. There's also a game that involves one person sitting down, pretending to cook or do something, and other people ask them, "Do you have any daughters?" They answer, "No, you're not going to touch my daughters!" Then all the others, each holding onto the back of the next one, try to catch the daughter. When people in the line fall down everybody laughs.

Undated

We're at Matshiteu. I really loved this gathering and now it's over. There were Innu from all over and we all had a good time. There's only one thing I didn't like. I thought we'd act quickly to continue our fight to protect the land, but that's not what happened.

We'll try to do something in two weeks' time, but if I could find some supporters, I'd act in a split second. If I could just find a few women to help me.

October 1

This is about my sister Maniaten. I miss her so much. She still comes out to support us if we have a protest or a meeting—she always comes—but she really isn't well. I've heard her talk so often about life in nutshimit long ago. She loved it so much and had such respect for the land. When we lived on the land we didn't need money; we were self-sufficient. After Maniaten married, she still spent most of her time in nutshimit. She believes it's vital for us to be there and to respect our land. She was always so proud and strong, she had such self-respect, but now she's sick and it's so hard for her to do anything. I really miss being able to rely on her.

October 14

Sometimes I wonder what the Innu are waiting for. The situation is already so unacceptable. I'm starting to feel scared as well as frustrated. I'll need to try harder to wake the women up. I really miss the times when they showed their power to the world.

Nin Tshaukuesh

October 19

My daughter Ishkueu, I want to tell you what I think of you. I love you so much and I feel such tenderness for you in my heart, as I do for all my children. There's something else I want to say to you. I want to thank you for keeping your baby. It was your decision. I thought my husband would help me to keep our granddaughter, so when I heard he wasn't going to help, I felt betrayed. I

Tshaukuesh preparing caribou leg. Photo: Penashue family collection.

Maniaten. Photo: Peter Sibbald.

Margaret Cornfoot. Photo: Peter Sibbald.

was also very upset that we were the only ones who wanted to fight for your child's future. I've watched you and I see how much you love your children. It warms my heart to know how well you care for them, and this must also make you very happy in your own heart. A while ago we talked about my ways, and I told you how caring for my children and hearing their words of encouragement makes me feel so good. I hope you'll find something good in what I say. I know you'll always take good care of your children. Thank you.

From your mother, Tshaukuesh

October 30

I'm leaving for Montreal.[27]

What will we talk about when we speak? We've been saying the same thing for so many years, but the government isn't listening. I believe all the women on earth should take a stand, because our governments have made us endure too much. We'll continue with our struggle. We aren't the only ones who want to defend our rights. All the Indigenous peoples on earth are struggling, and so are the Uinipaunnu. We must protest and do all that we can so the governments will stop killing people, our grandfathers, our grandmothers, our fathers and mothers, stop violating them and making the children cry. When the government representatives came here on tour, I spoke out, and this is what I said: "I hope the government stops causing us harm."

Nin Tshaukuesh

November 13

Trip to Toronto and Whitby

Today we were invited over by a friend, a woman named Margaret.[28] While we're here, she wants us to visit the land that she's trying to protect against people who want to destroy it by chopping down all the trees and building on it. They want to save their land from development and keep it safe for the animals. They're holding demonstrations like the ones we organize, and the women with Margaret all help each other out a lot. We're

Snowshoe. Photo: Camille Fouillard.

Shadows and ice on tent wall. Photo: Camille Fouillard.

very happy to see her so involved. She was our first ally when the women of Sheshatshiu began to organize our protests, and she helped us a lot. Now she's fighting for her own land.

Nin Tshaukuesh

November 14

I want to talk about the hearings they had here in Sheshatshiu with the Innu people and their leaders. It was a lot of hard work. I want to explain the reasons for organizing these events. The Akaneshau from the government organized their tour, looking for allies to help them destroy the Innu. Now they'll review their findings, and then they'll decide whether to recommend the continuation of military training on Innu territory.[29] The announcement will be made soon, around Christmas time.[30] This is why the Innu are holding their own hearings, too. We need to find allies to help us—anyone, no matter if they're Akaneshau or Innu. We need a lot of support if we want to put an end to the military training. Our land is everything to us and so is our culture. We must not lose it.

Nin Tshaukuesh

November 14

Kanani, I want to tell you what I think. I was very sorry when you began to work, but what could I do about it? I see you walk outside to your car. You're well-dressed and you look so elegant as you drive away. I want you to know how much I miss you since you took this job. Now you won't be able to go on the land, you who loved nutshimit so much and who used to help me do all the work that needed to be done. You won't be able to take your children to nutshimit, either. It seems you're always working, and I'm afraid you've abandoned forever the way of life that you loved so much in nutshimit. This is what's on my mind when I think of you. I love you and all my children very much. I wish I could have you all with me always because I love you so much. I miss you terribly.

It's me, your mother.

November 28

I, Elizabeth Penashue, would like to talk to all of you who helped us when we were arrested for trying to defend our land. I thank you for all your support. We must never lose hope. Please continue to support us in defending our rights against those who want to destroy us, like the Akaneshau government. I'm happy that we've opened our eyes, that we've come together in unity to be strong. Most importantly, you too must continue to confront the government.

Nin Tshaukuesh

Don McKenzie, I hope everything will go your way for Christmas and New Year, and for your wife and children. I thank you.

1995

March 20

Today we left to go on another speaking tour.

March 22, Six Nations

Today we went to a school to show the children our film.[31] After we showed the film I spoke, and then we went to another school. In the evening around seven o'clock we went to see a First Nations film. I went by myself because my friend was sick.

March 23

We're back at the school. Mani-Katinen has started to speak. Sometimes I get the urge to laugh because sometimes she says "shit" by mistake. Once she's done speaking, it's my turn to talk.

March 24

This morning we went to the tent where the Indigenous people were praying.

Now we're at Sheila Copps's constituency office in Hamilton, protesting. She's the Minister for the Environment. There are already a lot of people gathered to support us and others still coming. The sun is shining brightly on us.

Tonight we'll speak at the church, where there should be a big crowd. One of our friends delivered a long speech, very supportive of the Innu. That's what Mani-Katinen and I did today.

Once we finished speaking, we left for Toronto. I met my son Makkes at Kari's house, where we're staying. I was so happy to see him. He helps me a lot.

March 25

This afternoon we need to get to the place where we'll be speaking, and we have to get something to eat. Tonight we're going to see Kashtin.

March 26

This morning we're leaving to meet Rick Cober Bauman.[32] We'll be speaking in his church.

March 28

We made our presentation and everything went very well. There were some Indigenous people there.

March 29

This morning we made our first presentation at the school, then went to the government building where we met with deputy ministers. This is what we did. That's all.

Nin Tshaukuesh

March 30

We're going home today. We've been gone for two weeks, and I'm very relieved to be done. This is the first time there were just two of us, with no one to translate or help us. We did everything in our power to help each other out when we were presenting and we took turns, Mani-Katinen and I, Tshaukuesh. During our trip, there were times when I felt very distressed as I thought of all the things the government has done to the Innu. This is why we came on this tour, to tell people about that. We're also hoping to build our network and find more supporters who can help us fight to protect our culture and our animals.

Sometimes it amazes me to see how far the women have come and our determination to do everything in our power. Sometimes, though, I also feel I'm not up to the task. I wish we could find an Innu woman who can speak very good English to help us.

April 5

I'm on the plane this morning, approaching the other side of the ocean, on our way to England. The time here is just after eight o'clock, but in Sheshatshiu it's only four. It's very beautiful up here in the air. I haven't stopped praying during the whole flight. I also prayed for the other Innu on this trip, that the Creator would give us courage.

After the plane took off, I thought about our campaign. I'm prepared to give everything I have to defend our Innu brothers and sisters, our children, our grandchildren, and our land. So why am I so afraid of flying? I'm not a crowd of people, just myself alone, and there are so many people I want to protect and defend, including many children. It's daunting. We've lost so much, and many more will die because of what they're doing to our land. That's why I'm so committed to doing this work.

This is all for now, because we're about to land. I'll write more later.

Nin Tshaukuesh

Bush House, BBC World Service, Program: *Newshour*

It's evening already, and my son Peter is being interviewed by journalists. This morning we went to the office of the man we're staying with and talked to some Akaneshau. Then we had a nap, and the weather had turned nasty by the time they woke me up.

April 6

There's a lot of support for the Innu here. This morning the man we're staying with told us they were going to try to climb up and put a flag on Nelson's Column in Trafalgar Square. He told us not to look at the police but just wait and see what would happen. Manian, Peter, Mani-Katinen, Thea, and I were all there. We all tried to act as though nothing was happening, and after a while there was a big crowd. The Englishmen who did it told us they'd tried to do something similar before but the wind was so strong they couldn't attach the banner, so this time they made it with netting so it wouldn't catch the wind so much. Once the flag was up, there were police everywhere, but it was too late and they couldn't do anything. I wish our people could have seen how brave those Englishmen were and how smart to figure out how to do it. We hope they won't go to jail; we didn't see the police do anything to them.[33]

Nin Tshaukuesh

April 7

This morning the journalists arrived early to interview Peter, Mani-Katinen, and me. We were very pleased they came and glad to share our information with them.

At four o'clock this afternoon we left for Lancaster by train. We'll speak with journalists there too, and on Tuesday we'll catch the train again.

Nin Tshaukuesh

April 8, Carlisle

This morning we left again by train. It was only an hour to our first stop. We climbed down and were taken to a place where there are a lot of stores so we could look around at all the things being sold.

April 9

Since we left Sheshatshiu and arrived in England, I've been wanting to write about how I see things and what I'm feeling. Everything is so different here. Sometimes I feel as though I'm stuck in a hole and I'll never be able to escape. The buildings are so big you can't see the horizon and there's no fresh air to breathe. There's no land, only concrete, and no water. I've never seen a lake here, and it seems there's pollution everywhere. It's as if we're surrounded by clouds, and people drive like crazy, so many vehicles and so fast. It's very dangerous. Whenever we're in the car, they're honking their horns. Sometimes the noise of the tshishkuteutapan makes me jump. I'm always scared. I never feel right except once in a while when we get to go outside a

"Canada: Let the Innu Live"—Climbers on Nelson's Column. Photo: Survival International.

bit to see the land and the rivers. It's true that we do get out sometimes, but I really don't like being in a foreign country. I really wonder how the English people can like living in this place.

Nin Tshaukuesh

Shrewsbury

We're back here again. We had to change trains and we must have looked funny, running as fast as we could to jump on the train. We almost missed our connection. We were laughing and scared at the same time. I just had to mention this little adventure.

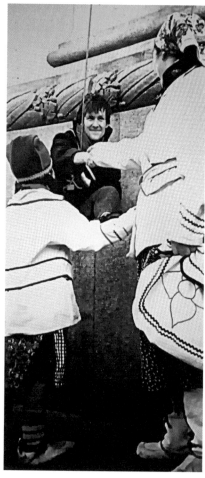

April 10, Swansea

We arrived here around noon. Peter has already been interviewed, and soon it will be our turn. After supper, we'll go back to the conference. Then there'll be a dance, and then our work will be done. That's all.

April 13

We're travelling again. Our plane took off from St. John's and we've already reached the other side of Pakua-shipu. I thank the Creator that we've been able to finish this work that took us so far away to England.

April 22

I'm writing to Mani-Mat. This is Tshaukuesh. How are you doing? I hope you're doing okay. I'm on board a plane as I write to you and I'm scared of flying, but I don't want to hurt the feelings of the women who invited me by telling them how hard this is for me—that wouldn't be respectful. I'll be very happy when this gathering of women is done. I was reading my prayer book and when I was done praying, I said to myself, "I'll write to Mani-Mat." I'm travelling with a very nice woman from Utshimassit named Tshaki. We're approaching Halifax, which is a comfort to me. There's something else I wanted to say to you. I wanted to thank you for coming with me on the trip and for all your help. I hope you're not getting discouraged, not giving up on helping the people who still want to keep up the struggle to defend ourselves and our land. Even when we suffered, we never got discouraged. Even when we had to leave our children behind, we tried to stay strong. I will never forget. We also know what the future will look like for our children and our grandchildren, how much they'll suffer if we don't succeed. There are so many things that you've helped make possible for me.

   Nin Tshuakuesh

Tshaukuesh and her granddaughter Thea (Penashue) and daughter-in-law Manian watch as one of the climbers, Jerry Moffatt, descends from the column.
Photo: Penashue family collection.

Tshaukuesh and Thea shake hands with Jerry. Photo: Penashue family collection.

April 22

I'm writing to you from my seat on the plane, my daughter Ishkueu. I want to thank you for making me so proud of you. You're so skilled at managing things, and at caring for your children. You're so brave and competent. I remember one time we were scared of a moose, and then I heard you and your sister Kanani organizing everyone. We all followed your instructions and everything turned out fine. And then when we wanted to go picking berries and there was no babysitter, you said to your father, "Why don't you take the little kids with you and we'll take the older ones?" And he did just what you asked. Everything went well, and we got lots of redberries. There's something else I want to say to you about when you went to nutshimit with your children. I was so happy about all the help you gave me with my work, and how well you cared for the children, and your brothers and sister too, how loving you are. They were so happy when they heard you were coming, and so was I. I wanted to have all my chores done so you'd be pleased. I wanted to make your tent nice and comfortable and set up the hammock for your children so they could swing. I cleaned up all around the outside of the tent so you'd like the way it was all set up. I wanted to do everything I could to make you happy, because you've given me so much joy in my heart by coming to nutshimit. I often think, "My daughter is really following in my footsteps." This is what I think of you.

There's just one thing that upsets me that I wanted to let you know about. It's to do with your daughter Pishum. I keep hoping that you'll change your mind and have her baptized. Maybe you just haven't had the time to do it, but I've been waiting patiently for you to get it done. That's all. I love you, all my children.

We're landing in Winnipeg.

Nin, your mother

Elizabeth P.

April 30

Today we came to nutshimit in the area of Iatuekupau. It's a beautiful spot here. After they dropped us off, Francis and our sons went back to fetch the canoes from Enipeshakimau, and I went into the bush to find the best spot to make a fire for a cup of tea.

May 2

This morning we got up very early to take advantage of this time of day when the snow is still hard to help Peter set up his tent. I'll go find boughs for the floor while Francis cuts the tent poles.

My son Pineshish killed a water bird. He was very happy and so was I. After he brought it to us, he left again with Kaputshet and Napeu.

May 7

We arrived here at Shapeshkashu yesterday. Today we got up at six o'clock and ate our breakfast. My husband said, "You should cook the duck we got," so I thought, "I won't go get boughs then." I plucked the bird and singed it and started cooking. Then I made some yeast bread and bannock. Once everything was cooked, we all ate together. Then we all helped to move the tent, and I thanked Peter and Manian for their help. It took no time at all before we were moved and settled again.

May 8

This morning after breakfast Francis left to walk along the shore, but he didn't get any game. In the meantime, we were looking for a sikuaskua to hang the pot up. Peter and Manian and the children chopped wood. This is what we've been doing since we came to nutshimit. We never have any spare time at all, because there's always something to do.

Nin Tshaukuesh

May 12

The men left early to go duck hunting. It must have been around five o'clock when they got up.

May 20

We started off this morning by going to check our net. My sons and five of our grandchildren—Kaputshet, Megan, Nikashantess, Napeu, and Thea—came with my husband and me. After we got back, we set out in the canoe again to find a new spot for our camp, and then we prepared the site. Pineshish helped his father by clearing the snow while I packed it down with my feet to make the tent base. Once that work was done, I said to myself, "I'll go to the marsh and get boughs." The route I took to the marsh reminded

me of all the times I picked bakeapples there.[34] I crossed the marsh and went into the woods on the other side where I saw a stand of fir trees. My two dogs were tagging along behind me, and one of them was a long time coming out of the woods. All of a sudden, I saw something move in a tree and I thought it was a porcupine. I watched it as I approached, because I wanted to get it. Once I could see it clearly, I called out to Peter. All the children came too, and Pineshish started to chop down the tree. I felt so happy, watching him swing the axe with such strength and energy. He had almost chopped his way through the whole tree before it fell to the ground, and then they killed the porcupine and we went back to the camp. When we got there, I said to them, "We'll give this one away." This is what we did, and we were very glad to be able to share.

Nin Tshaukuesh

May 23

Awful weather—it rained all night. It's stopped now but the fog has come in. I can't wait for the sun to come out again. The children went to check their net and they got a trout. They were so happy and proud of themselves. Seeing their excitement made me very happy too.

Nin Tshaukuesh

May 27

This morning we went to get our luggage that we'd left behind when we relocated. When we got back, we unpacked and organized the tent. Then the children went fishing and Kaputshet caught his first fish—after he reeled it in the others all wanted to try too. He was so excited about the fish, I could imagine what was going on in his mind, how happy he must be. I cleaned it right away. It was a beautiful fish with red flesh and lots of fat. Since we've been in nutshimit I feel so much joy and satisfaction, and such appreciation for this life here.

Nin Tshaukuesh

Making Innu doughnuts. Photo: Chris Sampson.

Roast duck. Photo: Penashue family collection.

Kaputshet with fish and dog. Photo: Penashue family collection.

May 28
Life is good. We're going to build a fire and cook a meal together. The sun is shining, and the children love it here. While we were searching for a good place to make the fire, we spotted pineu, but none of us had a rifle. The children started throwing stones at them and Francis caught one that way. He was actually shouting and jumping up and down with excitement at his success. We made our fire and other friends arrived, so we started cooking: roast duck on a spit and fried fish, and I made doughnuts. And then we feasted. After we ate, we relaxed for a while, and then they took the children back to camp by canoe while the rest of us said the rosary together. There was a cemetery near where we built our fire, so we prayed for our ancestors. I'd been hoping to come back and pray here and was so happy to have had the chance to do that.

June 4
This morning I got up very early to do something special for Kaputshet's birthday. First I had to prepare the yeast to make bread. Then I did some cooking, keeping an eye on the yeast because I wanted to bake a beautiful cake with the dough. My daughter Ishkueu helped me by looking after the children, and Shimieu, Manian's father, also cooked some fish. After supper, we ate the Innu yeast cake and jello, and sang to Kaputshet and took some pictures. He was thrilled that we celebrated his birthday.
    Nin Tshaukuesh

June 6
We're headed to Kamit. It's very sad to be leaving nutshimit but it's time to go. We'll come again when the warm weather returns next spring. We're so carefree out here; our health is good and the children are well-behaved. At night, they're already asleep at nine or ten o'clock, and they always sleep really well.

June 11, In Sheshatshiu
This morning my daughter Ishkueu told me about her dream: "We were in nutshimit, and I saw a muskrat. Pineshish was sitting by the edge of the water and he yelled out, 'Get a gun!' He really didn't want to kill the muskrat, so it swam over to him and circled around in the water next to Pipitsheu. He was

happy and he took the muskrat and brought it into the tent. You were doing some sewing in the tent and you came to see it and took it from him, feeling sorry for it because it had been bitten and was badly hurt. The children were all sorry for it too."

This is a very important dream and a beautiful dream for Ishkueu.

June 15, Here in Sheshatshiu

Today we had a real fright, because the bush plane carrying my husband had to make an emergency landing. They weren't hurt but the plane was a little beat up. However, they managed to reach a river before it came down, so they were able to land on the water instead of crashing in the woods. My husband and the pilot were very frightened. That's all for this story.

Nin Tshaukuesh

June 17

We arrived in Halifax at a quarter after one in the afternoon and were met by Betty Peterson. We spoke at the People's Summit at St. Mary's University about low-level flying and the situation in Emish.[35] David Suzuki also spoke.

June 18

Elizabeth, Mani-Mat, and Betty. We had breakfast, and left Halifax at ten for the airport, arriving just in time to get on the plane for Goose Bay.

June 22

Today a woman from Utshimassit and I are going to Winnipeg to a women's meeting. I imagine there'll be a crowd there. I'm not very happy about it because I have so much to do, and I don't really like leaving my children and grandchildren.

Nin Tshaukuesh

June 23

We're in Winnipeg, and the talks are already underway. A man is addressing the crowd, a very good speaker, very powerful. I really wish there was a radio transmitter here with me, so I could broadcast what he's saying. When he finished, a woman rose and spoke. She could barely contain her sobbing as she told him how beautiful his speech was.

Nin Tshaukuesh

June 24

We're still in Winnipeg. The last meeting will be held tomorrow and we leave on Monday. Today we're listening to the Elders speak. The words of the women are very inspiring. "We can't be worrying about what others are doing. We need to focus on what we need to do ourselves," one of them said. "It's up to each of us in our own community to set up a shelter for children with no one to care for them. These children have so much hardship in their lives. The parents are drinking, leaving their children all over the place. If we can set up homes for them, they'll have somewhere to go."

June 25

The meeting is going very well. The women are really strong, and there are many of us speaking out. Everyone I've heard so far makes so much sense. I've also come to know that there are Indigenous peoples everywhere and they live the same way we do. And like us, they're being abused and mistreated by the government, but since they've woken up they too are standing up and speaking out. There's something else I want to talk about. I spoke to one of the women in charge and said, "I want to show my films," and she responded, "Okay, I'll make sure they're screened." I was so happy and grateful that she accepted my request. If only you knew how this made me feel in my heart! Finally, the time came for me to show them and speak. I talked about the way the government has been treating us and after I finished, I saw that quite a few women were crying and they said, "We want to help you in any way we can." Quite a few of them asked me for my address and information about my films. I feel so grateful to these women who want to support us.

Nin Tshaukuesh

June 26

We're on our way back to Sheshatshiu, happy to be going home after our meeting with the women. We've flown over so many places since the plane took off, we must be over Esker by now. We thank the Creator for our return home. Now I'll have to find a way to help the Innu and also to tell the women what happened at the meetings. I wish I could just work quietly. I need to be careful that I don't end up exhausting myself.

Nin Tshaukuesh

July 20

I'm back in Sheshatshiu and I want to write about what I think. I've been really upset now for two weeks, bothered by a number of things. I won't be able to write about all of them, but one of them has to do with my children and grandchildren and my love for them. Another is where all the strong women of Sheshatshiu have gone. It seems as though they don't care anymore—they've been crushed. The men have started to ignore us again, the way they did in the past. If you ask me, if the women don't rise up they'll be treated badly. There's no reason for us to get discouraged, because we've been incredibly strong, but I don't like that we're being ignored. It's very upsetting.

August 7

I'm writing this on the train to Uashat, thinking about my ancestors travelling here on foot and by canoe. I'm looking out at the Mishta-shipu, where I often paddled with my parents as a child. There were many rapids, some of them very dangerous, and big mountains. It's a winding river, so they often had to stay close to shore or make a portage, carrying all their gear until they could safely get back into their canoes again. There must have been swarms of blackflies and mosquitoes too, and people with large families probably had to cope with two canoes as well as all their gear. But to compensate, their campsites were always in beautiful locations, and once they reached the highlands it was easier, though they still had many challenges. That was their way of life. They never complained. They never gave up.

September 11

Me, Tshaukuesh; Mani-Katinen, Anne R., Tshanet Pun, Mani-Mat Hurley, Nuisha Penashue, An-Mani Andrew, Shanimen Andrew, Ishkueu Asimin, Nush M., a chief, and four Akaneshau women. I really liked that there were so many of us at this women's meeting. I'm so glad it went well.

Nin Tshaukuesh

September 24

Here in Net,[36] in the territory of the Aiassimeut. Soon we'll be heading out to the part of our land that's being destroyed by mining, an area belonging to both Innu and Inuit. There are a lot of people here, Innu and Inuit. Some travelled here by boat, and the elders and some others came by helicopter. They gathered us together and brought us to a place where we could talk about the negotiations that are taking place.

September 27

We left the Aiassimeut territory on Friday. There was a meeting, and on Sunday we were taken to Emish where they're doing mining explorations. There was a crowd of us: Sheshatshiu Innu, Aiassimeut, and Utshimassit Innu. This is the second time I've travelled to Emish. The first time I went there were just a few buildings, but now it's grown a lot. The government is talking about building an airport, a wharf for big boats, hotels, stores, houses. This is breaking my heart. Never again will we see all that was on this land, all the life and the good things it held. The trees will be cut down, the lakes and mountains will all be changed, and the animals will be gone. Nutshimit and the animals that live there are how the Innu and the Aiassimeut survive. I feel so sad for the children. We won't be able to save any of this land for them to raise their children the way we raised them.

October 22

Kanani lost her baby boy, Mikaniss. Everybody is heartbroken, weeping—nobody could do anything to save him. Maybe the Creator wanted that baby in a shining place of light, in one of the mansions Jesus talked about. I hope that's where he's gone, to a beautiful place.

This morning I woke up early and I decided to write my journal. I couldn't sleep because I'm thinking so much about my grandson, so many things. When I was trying to sleep last night, I heard somebody knocking on the door, a light little sound as if the baby was knocking at the door of the Creator's house. I thought it must be my grandson and they must have let him into Heaven. Then I went back to sleep feeling comforted. But it's hard to lose a child, to be unable to raise him into the person he would have become. I feel so sad for my daughter and her partner.

Canoeing in traditional clothing near Sheshatshiu. L–R: Shuash Nuna, Mani-Katinen Nuna, Tshaukuesh, Francis. Photo: Innu Nation Archive.

"We're always thinking about them, our children and grandchildren." Tshaukuesh with her granddaughters Uapshish and Manteu Iskueu. Photo: Penashue family collection.

Tshaukuesh (on the right) with a group of children. L–R, top: Manteu Pone, Brad Puiash, Manteu Iskueu Pone. L–R, bottom: Christa Penunsi, Lizette Nuna, Edwina Nuna. Photo: Penashue family collection.

October 24

This morning I was gathering together some things to send to people who are on the road. While I was organizing the things, my grandson Nikashantess came in and said, "Are we going to nutshimit?" I felt so sorry I couldn't take him there. I was surprised that he'd ask me this, such a beautiful question.

Nin Tshaukuesh

November 16

Here in Sheshatshiu. I want to say what I'm thinking. Caring for my grandchildren is exhausting. I have no time to do anything else, no help looking after them and doing so much housework. At night when the children have gone to bed, I think about all the things I need to do, but I never seem to get around to doing them. I barely have the energy to take a bath, I'm so weary. I find this very hard sometimes, and when the weather is good I long to be outside.

It's very difficult to have grandchildren, especially when you can't find the strength to say no, to say, "I can't look after them." No matter how tired I am I still say yes, in spite of myself. The only thing that matters is the love I feel for them. They're like my own children, and I want to care for them in the same way.

But I need to look after myself too.

Nin Tshaukuesh

November 21

Emma Milley

Tshaukuesh Penashue

Nuisha Penashue

Pinamin Penashue

Two Akaneshau women (Lyla Andrew and Kari Reynolds)

And four men:

Utshesh Nuna

Apenam Pone

Peter Penashue

Kanikuen Andrew

These are the people who are in jail. We're waiting to find out what they're going to do to us. Maybe they'll transfer us to another jail, but I'm hoping we'll stay here. Our families may be able to visit us if we stay closer to home. We're always thinking about them, our children and grandchildren. But whatever hardship comes our way, we must still be strong to protect our children's futures. That's why we're here in this prison.

I'm happy to see so many women here. I'm feeling stronger now that I've listened to them, and their strength gives me courage.

November 21

They separated us. I'm with Pinamin Penashue, and Nuisha Penashue is in a different cell. Emma Milley is here too, in a different cell, and the Akaneshau women. But we can hear each other if we call out. When they lock the cells you feel really bad, as if you're suffocating, because everything is made of concrete and there's only a very small opening in the door—just a hole to put food through and a tiny peephole so they can see us. The toilet is right there in your room, which is undignified and disgusting when you're eating. The beds are uncomfortable, very hard with plastic mattresses. One blanket. Very cold at night. If you ask for another blanket they bring you a plasticized one—not very comforting, but I took it anyway because I was so cold. After we got here we were very hungry and thirsty, but when we asked for something to drink, the woman who brought it acted as though she was afraid of us and she gave us warm water. We were so thirsty. Why would she treat us like that?

When we left home this morning, we didn't have time to eat because we were rushing to get ready for the protest. We knew we'd be going to jail so we wanted to do laundry, feed the children, get everything in order. That's why we're so hungry now. I found it very hard knowing I'd be leaving the children and grandchildren to go to jail. When there's no mother in the house, the children are lonely.

Nin Tshaukuesh

November 23

Still in jail. We called Tinien Ashini and Peter Penashue to talk about what we should do. We were a bit confused and indecisive; some wanted to go home and some wanted to stay, but eventually we all decided to stay and we felt good about the decision. We're getting stronger.

We are Innu women. We told the Akaneshau women we were going to stay in jail. We wouldn't sign the documents they wanted us to sign. Now we're waiting to be transferred to Stephenville, far from home. Why don't they stop what they're doing to us? The abuse has gone on long enough. Now they're putting women in jail. We miss all our children and grandchildren; I'm worried about all of them. Since I got here I'm so anxious I can't sleep properly, and I feel dizzy and achy when I get up. I don't want to tell the other women this in case it makes them anxious too. I always try to be strong.

Nin Tshaukuesh

November 24

Holding my children and grandchildren in my heart. I'm an Innu woman, a mother and grandmother. I'm used to being my own boss; nobody orders me around. This is my land, our land to protect for future generations. It's insane to put me in jail when I didn't do anything wrong. Why did they do it? They should have stayed where they came from, on their own land. How many times have we said, "Leave us alone! Stop what you're doing to us! Even if you don't stop what you're doing to our land, you won't change us or our way of life. Our

Snow scene. Photo: Navarana Igloliorte.

Tshaukuesh and Manteu tobogganing. Photo: Elizabeth Yeoman.

ways are very different from your ways." They think they know everything, and they believe their way of life is better. The Innu have been fighting the government for so long now with protests, placards, and meetings, and they don't like it but if they won't stop, neither will we.

November 25

This morning at eight they let me out of the cell for the whole day until eight in the evening. I feel a little bit better. They let me go outside for half an hour, then to the exercise room, then we had knitting, then supper at five, then more knitting. Today was the first day I could get outdoors and move around a little. When I was in jail before, I could move around more. Maybe that's why I feel so sick this time, just lying down all the time. I ask the Creator to let me sleep well and take away my pains, fatigue, and anxiety. I'm so worried about my children, so far away.

Nin Tshaukuesh

November 26

Still here in jail with the other Innu women. I called home and everything is okay there. I find it very hard to call Sheshatshiu, but I did. I hope they weren't upset after I hung up.

This afternoon Pinamin Penashue and I went to church in the basement. The Akaneshau were singing and I understood a bit of the song. It made me cry: Jesus loves the little children. I felt so lonely, so homesick. It hurts, but we should stop crying. In the old days, Innu people didn't have jails and never imagined they'd ever go to jail. We thought we'd always be free to do whatever we wanted to do. We didn't know what the government was or where it was, or anything about it. We never dreamed they would come and destroy our land and hurt our people. It's wrong!

November 28

I don't feel so strong anymore because all we do is sit around all day. I'm weak from being inside all the time with no chance to go walking. Sometimes they let us go outside but not for long—just half an hour, not enough.

December 1

We got home yesterday. When we got in to the airport in Goose Bay, my husband and my children and grandchildren all came to meet me. I was overjoyed to see them all. Only one thing is still worrying me. One of my grandchildren is sick. She doesn't look well at all. Anyway, we're back in Sheshatshiu.

Nin Tshaukuesh

December 9

Today we're at a meeting about the development at Emish. The Akaneshau want to hear what the elders have to say. It's going to be a big meeting, very important. We're thinking about what to say. Our way of life is at stake.

An Innu woman from Uashat is speaking; her name is Utusimash. She has seen a lot and remembers how the land was destroyed and how the government tricked the people in the past. What she has to say is very important because she remembers a long way back.

Nin Tshaukuesh

December 14

Why didn't the government explain to the people how much this development would damage our land? They should have asked us first. It's Innu and Inuit land. They don't worry about us, they just take what they want without asking. They don't care that the land and the animals are everything to us.

Nin Tshaukuesh

December 22

The Innu have immense knowledge of nutshimit and this is why it's so important to us to safeguard our land. We've endured so much in our struggle. They're dropping bombs on our land.

1996

February 9

This morning Peter's baby was born. A lovely chubby baby with lots of hair. We're all very happy except that her mother, Manian, is still recuperating because of the Caesarean. But she's doing okay. And the little stranger has arrived in Sheshatshiu. When she got here she called out to us:

> *I was born today. I'm Pipun, the little stranger girl.*
>
> *Nika Manian, I want to tell you that I'm sorry you went through so much pain to have me. Even though it was the doctors who did the Caesarean, you're still the one who gave me life. When you woke up after the surgery, you were in pain, but I could see you were happy when you saw me. You didn't blame me. You just loved me. I love you too, Nika, and I'll love you all my life.*
>
> *Soon we left the hospital and now I'm here in Sheshatshiu. The first thing I did when I got here was to look for the other children. I called out but nobody answered. I called again and again: "Where are you? Are you there?" Then I saw them, but they all looked miserable so I was frightened and I wondered what would become of me. Where can I find a healthy life? I'm Pipun, Mandishkuess, the little stranger girl in a new world. I wish I'd been born long ago into the good life of my ancestors, but instead I'm born into sorrow and despair.*

This is Tshaukuesh. I wrote the above in the voice of Pipun, my granddaughter. I wrote this story for her because so many things have changed now. The children used to be happy—no alcohol, no drugs. Our lives were good. I hope she'll understand this story when she's grown up. I call this story Sheshikan.

Nin Tshaukuesh

February 24

It's evening and I'm in the tent. I miss my children. Some of them are away getting an education, some are at work. I know they need jobs and money, but they should also think about our traditions and protecting the land. I feel they're only looking in one direction and they don't care if they lose our culture. They were so happy in nutshimit, but now they don't want to go anymore. I'm afraid for them when I think about the healthy food, the happy way of life they're losing.

Nin Tshaukuesh

February 27

It's an anxious time with an election coming, because some people start drinking. Sometimes they bribe the young people with money for alcohol and drugs. The election hasn't even been declared yet but they've started already.

An election causes a lot of problems, but there is one good thing about it: people are energized. Before they started talking about an election, everybody was apathetic, they stayed home and nobody showed up for meetings. Now people are on the move, excited, dynamic—though I do worry that some of them just want alcohol and drugs. Still, I wish our people would have this kind of energy all the time. That's what I think.

March 1

A priest I really trusted, Father Fred Magee, got sick and died. I never missed any of the other priests when they were gone, but Father Magee helped me many times. I shared everything with him, everything that hurt so much inside. I never felt shy when I talked to him. I could tell him anything. I didn't realize he was so ill.

There was one thing I used to wonder about though: Why did he sometimes smile when I told him sad stories? I never got a chance to ask him that, and now I never will. Maybe it was because he thought if he smiled it would make it less painful. Or maybe he wanted to be positive. Or perhaps he laughed because he felt helpless. I should have gone to see him and asked him about that before he died. But he's gone now. Our priest is gone.

Sometimes he would visit us in the morning for breakfast or a cup of tea, and I didn't like it when he and my husband talked about the land. Later they started talking about protecting the land, but not in the way I thought they should do it. I wanted to organize meetings and protests. But Francis thought that was too extreme. He didn't really agree with what I was trying to do, and Kanani started to take her father's side, which really upset me. I wanted Francis to say, "Your mom is doing very important work. We should do more to support her. If we don't protect the land we'll have huge problems in the future. And your mom is a very strong woman who can lead us." I wanted them to believe in me.

March 2

My grandson Kaputshet and I went for a walk this afternoon. We got a ride along the Goose Bay road, and then we went into the woods and climbed the hill. When we got to where I wanted to go, we made a fire for tea and had a picnic, and then I told him stories about the priest who died. I said, "The good weather makes me happy. Maybe Father Magee gave us this beautiful day." Innu people believe that after people die they can still look down on us from Heaven. Then my grandson said to me, "Nukum, are we going to pray?" and I said, "Yes." We knelt down by the fire and I looked up to the sky and my grandson helped me to pray. I started crying and talking to Father Magee. I miss him so much. He wasn't like the other priests; he was kind and he helped people. When I finished praying we started walking again. I said to Kaputshet, "Look at that beautiful place over there—it's not too far—let's walk there." I found a big rock, round but split in two, like my broken heart. Before we left for home I took my axe and cut a blaze on a tree near the rock so I'd remember when I came back. The next time I come, I'll bring some paint to make some kind of mark or write something. My grandson had walked on ahead and he called out to ask me what I was doing, so I hurried to catch up with him. I asked him if he'd seen the rock and noticed the split. He was very quiet as he listened. That's all I have to say for today.

Nin Tshaukuesh

Toboggan and snowshoes. Photo: Melissa Tremblett.

March 30

Today I'm leaving for Toronto.[37] I'm just going by myself and I'm a bit nervous about it. I'll be on my own until Tuesday, and then I'm going to meet Peter and we'll go home together. I'm worried about my husband and I'm afraid for the children. I'm not sure if he'll look after them or just leave them alone. Before I left I said, "Please stay with the children! Look after them!" but he didn't say for sure that he would. I'll have to wait and see what happens. I wish he'd help me when I have to go away to speak. I wish I didn't have to worry about this so much, and I wish my husband would pray for me because I'm afraid of flying and I don't like to be alone. I'm going to pray for him too. As I write this I realize we must be close to our destination.

I hope everybody supports me.

Nin Tshaukuesh

April 2

My sister died, Maniaten Andrew, my eldest sister. We're all grieving, but we just have to accept it. It happens to everybody. Here's how I feel about her: I love all my sisters, but she was my favourite. She was such a good person, and so funny. She could make everybody laugh with her jokes. She was kind to everyone, never angry; even if she was displeased with people she never said anything and was still nice to them. She loved children. I remember when we were young I could see how devoted she was to her children and grandchildren and how hard she worked. She made sure the tent was always warm and cozy for the little ones. I remember her getting water from the lake and warming it on the stove to wash clothes. She kept everything so nice and clean—she worked endlessly until her children were grown up. Now she's finished her life's work. When she couldn't work anymore or even walk, she got really depressed and she talked often about nutshimit. She told me that when her grandchildren took her out for a drive, she would cry when she saw the lakes and the forest and couldn't walk there anymore. She said to me, "Tshaukuesh, I loved going out on the land with toboggans and snowshoes. I felt so proud to be out there walking across the frozen lakes, so happy to stop and make a fire and a pot of tea, or to set up camp in the evening. They're my best memories." The last words I said to her were "Good-bye. I love you, my sister. I love you so much. I'll always remember you and pray for you and your children

100

and grandchildren. I hope you'll be happy up there with the Creator. The Creator says it's time to come, and I know Heaven is a beautiful place. You're going to go through the big door of the Creator's home."

Nin Tshaukuesh

April 3

This was a hard trip. My son Peter had to bring me the sad news about Maniaten. I'm thinking about her children and grandchildren and praying for them. And I pray that the Creator will make me strong.

Nin Tshaukuesh

April 14

It's Sunday morning. Last night I had a nice dream about my mother. In the dream she said to me, "I heard you're a very strong woman, as strong as a man." I could hear her voice so clearly and I knew she was proud of me. That's all she said. It was a very short dream. It's the first time I've dreamed about my mother since she died.

Nin Tshaukuesh

April 26

We're in nutshimit at Minai-nipi. A helicopter came to our camp to bring my granddaughter from Sheshatshiu. She was there to have two teeth removed because she had a toothache. She was so glad to be back, and we were happy to see her too.

Early this morning the men went hunting, taking two children with them. Later in the afternoon they came back with two beavers, one mature and the other young. This will be our first beaver feast and we're looking forward to it very much.

Today we moved our camp to a new site. The weather was great. When we finished putting up our first tent, we stopped and ate duck for lunch. After lunch, we finished our work.

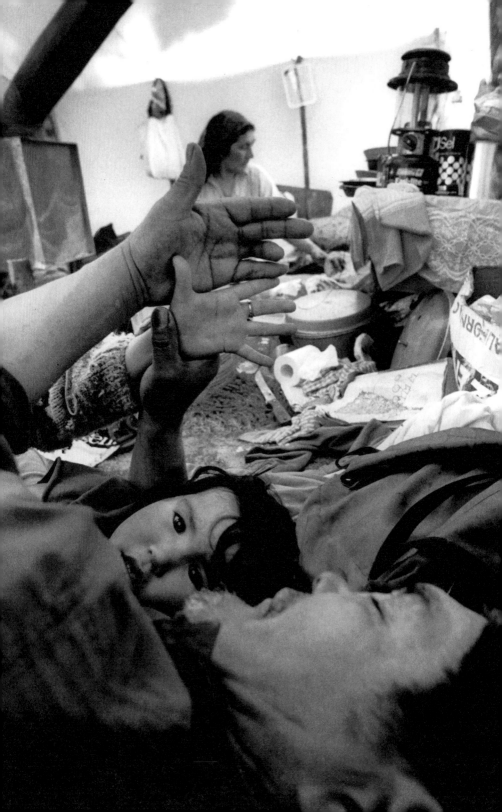

April 30

The men went goose hunting. They returned later in the evening with eight geese, which they shared with everybody in the camp. We were very happy the hunting went so well.

    Nin Tshaukuesh

May 3

Still at Minai-nipi. This afternoon the children and I went for a short walk along the shore and had a boil-up, which they really enjoyed. The men went hunting and killed one goose. Later in the day, the helicopter arrived bringing Tanien Ashini and some Akaneshau. That's all for today.

May 4

The Akaneshau journalists have been with us here in nutshimit for a week and they're heading home today.[38] There are others coming tomorrow.

May 8

We had visitors from the government of a country far away.[39] They came to hear from the Innu about how we're affected by the low-level flying. We gathered in one tent for the meeting. The visitors came in, and we explained to them how it frightens us and how the animals are affected by it too. We know the stress is bad for their health.

May 12

I'm expecting Kanani to come and see me here in nutshimit today. I'm working hard to clean up my tent, putting new boughs on the floor, but I haven't got enough yet. Two of my grandchildren are here: Makkes's daughter Kateri, and Megan. They know I need more boughs and they're talking about helping me get them. Makkes's daughter said, "Good idea! I love getting boughs in the woods with you." Then they went out and after a little while they came back with boughs. I was surprised at what Kateri said then: "Nukum, I went to get the boughs because I worry about you. You work so hard." I couldn't believe she would be so thoughtful at such a young age, five years old.

Francis and Pishum in nutshimit. Tshaukuesh in the background. Photo: Peter Sibbald.

May 18

My grandchildren and I are having so much fun hiking. I have seven of them with me, three girls and four boys, and my son Pineshish. When we first headed out on our trek, I wanted to go along the shore but they didn't like the idea, so we did what they wanted instead and climbed the hill. It was beautiful at the summit and we felt good. We made a fire and cooked lunch. I started making tea, but there was no stream or river nearby to cut ice from, so we melted snow.[40]

I feel healthier. Being in nutshimit is like good medicine.

May 20

We can't work outside because of the rainy weather. The only thing we did today was check the fishing net. We got some trout and some pike, which we cooked, and that's what we all ate. Afterward we all tried to work inside the tent.

May 21

This afternoon, my sons Peter, Makkes, and Tshak, and another guy, a cameraman, went by canoe along the open area between the ice and the shore. The rest of us stayed and enjoyed the time in our tent.

I've been so busy since we arrived here that I've hardly had a moment to pick up my journal. I was hoping to be able to write more often. However, I really enjoy all the work I do here and I do it with all my heart and strength. When my sons have gone hunting, I make bannock for them to eat when they stop for lunch and get supper ready for when they came back. Sometimes I think I won't finish in time, but somehow I always do. Often my hands are bleeding and painful from all the work, but I still feel so happy when I finish. It reminds me of when I was a young girl helping my parents.

June 3

We're going back to Sheshatshiu. I don't want to leave. I've felt my sister Maniaten's presence here in nutshimit every day and sensed her watching over us. The trees, the water, and the rivers all remind me of her and her love and respect for the land. I don't want to go—I had so many things still to do here.

Back in Sheshatshiu. I'd like to share my thoughts. There are many things that bother me, but I won't write them all down right now. The memories of nutshimit are still very fresh and I wish I was still there. When we arrived at our house in Sheshatshiu I opened the door and went inside and I felt so unhappy. I know my grandchildren did too, because one of them was crying.

I was very upset to see them looking so bored, and it seemed they couldn't find anything to do. I notice their expressions have changed. When they were in nutshimit there were so many things to occupy them, or they could go hunting with their dad or grandfather and stay out all day. The younger children played close by, or sometimes I took them on a hike and we had a boil-up or went canoeing. The children always slept well but this evening when I tried to put Pishum to sleep, she couldn't settle down. After a while I heard her screaming, so I ran to the bedroom and she looked so frightened lying there. I guess she had a nightmare. I lay down with her to comfort her. This is what Sheshatshiu does to us!!

Nin Tshaukuesh

July 19

We're on the train headed to Uashat, and I want to go to Sainte-Anne de Beaupré if I can find a babysitter. I also want to visit my daughter Ishkueu in North Bay, but not until Innu Nikamu is over. Then I'll take my children and husband with me. This is my summer holiday and I hope it all works out.

Nin Tshaukuesh

July 20

I really enjoy morning walks, but sometimes I don't have time because I can't find a sitter. I find it hard to leave my grandchildren with anybody I don't know well, because I think about all the child abuse that's been happening in our communities. I have a hard time with that whenever I want to go somewhere.

We arrived here in Ekuanitshu this evening from Sheshatshiu. I'm exhausted. I really need to have a nap, or maybe I should just go to bed already so I can feel like myself again.

Nin Tshaukuesh

August 2, Uashat

Innu Nikamu starts today. I'm so glad I decided to bring my children with me. I can see how much they're enjoying the festival. I hope everything goes well on my trip to visit my daughter and my friends. I'm really looking forward to it.

Nin Tshaukuesh

August 15

This morning Pineshish and I are leaving to go to North Bay to visit Ishkueu. This will be the first time travelling with Pineshish, and his first time flying on a big plane. He's very happy and excited and so am I. I'm trying to be strong and pretend that I'm not scared of flying. I explain about turbulence, how rough it might get when the plane lifts off or when it starts to descend, and what to do if something goes wrong on the flight.

Nin Tshaukuesh

August 18

We're back in Sheshatshiu. When we were in North Bay, we had bad news from home: my nephew was killed in a tragic accident; he was hit by a car. I felt so sorry for my sister, her husband, and her other children. It's very hard to accept but there was nothing we could do.

August 19

Here are my close relatives who have lost a family member:

Tuminik
An Pinamen Pokue
Tshani
Shimun
Shanimesh
Ipuan
Naunet R.
Atini N.
Animani
Animakunet
Nushis Penashue

Pien Kanikuen/Gregoire
Emit Nuna
Atuan Nuk/Nuke
Kanikuen R.
Shuaush Nuna
Shinipest Penashue

I'm thinking about my relatives. They'd be such strong people if they could stop drinking. If they ever needed my help, I'd try and help them as much as possible.

August 24

Sometimes I feel so troubled. I want to do so many things, but right now I don't have time for all of it because I'm taking care of my grandchildren so my daughter can go to school. For instance, I wish I had more time to write. However, I'll be happy and proud when I've finished this work of taking care of my grandchildren—my day is almost here.

October 6, Rotterdam

Tshak and I are going to speak about what the government is doing on our land.[41] I find it very, very hard to speak about these things. The last time we spoke I broke down. I want to be strong like Gandhi, to help my people, to help the children.

The government has done so much damage to our land! They made the dam at Patshishetshuanau and destroyed our hunting grounds. How many trees and animals have died? They killed them. And the low-level flying continues. So many things.

And another thing: it's very hard for me to go to so many places to speak. At home, you look after your children and grandchildren, you cook and clean up and do all those comforting homey things, but when you travel everything is different and strange. Even the time is different. It's morning in Sheshatshiu when it's evening somewhere else. It's hard to sleep when you're wondering what's going on at home. Too many things are strange.

October 7, Arnhem

My son and I are going to court to the trial of protesters who supported us by occupying runways here. We're going to talk about low-level flying and its effect on the animals. I'm trying to write down what I need to say, the stories I should remember when I speak.

. . .

The hearing is over. I'm amazed at what happened. While I was waiting for them to call me into the courtroom I was praying, and my prayers have been answered. I looked out the window and thought about the spirits of my parents and other people who have died, and I asked them to help me. When we entered the courtroom, I thought the judge looked like a good man. Sometimes he smiled and he seemed very kind. They called me to speak with Tshak to interpret. I made sure to speak very loudly and clearly so they'd pay attention, and also to build up my own confidence. I talked for quite a long time and I really appreciated Tshak's help. When we finished speaking we sat down, and the judge spoke. He said the protest was peaceful and the charges were dismissed. I kept on praying and looking out the window at the sky, feeling happy in my heart because I felt that everything I had done was coming together. The Creator had given me strength.

After the hearing, we took the train to Brussels. Now we're waiting for another train and I'm very tired. We've travelled so far and for so long.

Nin Tshaukuesh

October 8

This morning I went with Tshak and two Akaneshau to a government building to talk to some government representatives. First I met with one man and one woman, then we had tea and met with two men and a woman. They were well-dressed and looked very important. One of the men was bald. The other looked very nervous—I don't know why. Every time I tell the same story.

Nin Tshaukuesh

October 9, Brussels

This afternoon, we went to a protest at the Ministry of Defence. There were a lot of people and many reporters taking pictures and wanting to talk to us. Then we went to the government building, where we spoke to two men about low-level flying and our concerns about its impact on our land. They listened attentively; they didn't argue. Then they said they'd try to do something to support us.

This morning when I talked to the reporters they said they had heard about Sheshatshiu and that some Innu people are opposed to low-level flying but not all of them feel the same way. Tshak and I said, "Not one single Innu has said they were happy about low-level flying or that they don't care." We talked for a long time.

In the evening, we took the train again. We've finished the Belgian part of our trip and now we're going to Amsterdam. Tomorrow we don't have too much to do, not so much work, but we do have to meet some reporters at one. I can't believe we're here, so far from our home. It's amazing that we've come so far. How did I end up doing this?

October 10

We're still in Europe. We went on a small boat with the reporters. It's a very nice boat and I trust the woman who brought us here, but I'm not really happy to be so far from home. One reporter asked me what I think of it here and I said, "It's so built up you can't see the trees and the land. You can't feel the earth under your feet, only pavement."

I'm very, very tired every day but I have to do this to support my people, the children, the animals, and the land.

Nin Tshaukuesh

October 11, four thirty in the morning Sheshatshiu time

This is the last big thing I have to do. The Europeans and Tshak and I are going to put up a tent. I'm writing this on the train. We've changed trains once already, but we're not there yet. One more hour and we'll be there. We're exhausted. We've worked so hard and we're homesick. Tshak has fallen asleep. What we're doing is not easy but it is very, very important.

October 13

This morning after breakfast some people took us to see where the war was. We walked in the woods, and afterward we went to a military building and somebody took our picture. The place was closed to the public and surrounded by fences, but I stood outside and held up an Innu flag.

October 19

We got back from our trip two days ago. We stepped off the plane into a blizzard and the weather has been bad ever since; now it's rain mixed with snow, and high winds. Why is this happening? Maybe it's a bad omen. I watched the waves crashing into the rocks on the beach, close to the road. I haven't seen this kind of storm in a long time.

December 3

I was very happy about what the other women and I did. They said, "We should have another meeting on Tuesday, and before we start we should exercise a little." They thought the meeting went well. So we'll see how the next one goes.

    Nin Tshaukuesh

"The Europeans and Tshak and I are going to put up a tent."
Photo: Penashue family collection.

1997

February 7

This morning I was feeling really down until the phone rang and my little grandson Nikashantess answered it. I just stood there listening to hear what he'd say. He said, "Tshimue ma"—shut up—and hung up. I told him not to answer the phone again. When it rang again I answered and it was my husband. He told me that he was the one who called before. I never thought I'd laugh like that today when I was feeling so low this morning. Nikashantess is only four years old, and I thank him for cheering me up. I'm sharing this because I want him to read it some day and laugh about what he did. He's so funny.

    Nin Tshaukuesh

August 23

On the way to Natuashish and then on to Emish.[42] A lot of Innu and Inuit. The Aiassimeut were already here when we got here. First Aiassimeut, then Utshimassit Innu, then Sheshatshiu Innu. A lot of children. We came by boat to Utshimassit, then by plane from there. It took several days for everybody to get here with all their stuff. I got in on Saturday with Tanien Ashini and his girlfriend and their children, Penote Michel and his wife and children, Sam Nui, Shanimen Benuen, one Akaneshau, and one person from Utshimassit.

    Nin Tshaukuesh

August 25

Here in Emish, good weather, a lot of people camping, Utshimassit and Sheshatshiu Innu and Aiassimeut. This is the first time we all get together to fight the government. They're going to do more and more harm to the natural world, to our land and everything that lives on it. They can't just destroy everything.

August 26

Long ago the Innu didn't need money; they lived by their own work. Everything was pristine. The lakes, the woods, the land, mosses growing everywhere, flowers, grass—it was all so beautiful then.

August 28, Emish

Bad weather. Everybody's waiting to go home.

August 29

The weather is still down and we're all waiting. Maybe a helicopter can get in and take us to Utshimassit. We're all ready to go home; we miss our children and grandchildren.

"This is the first time we all get together to fight the government." Innu and Inuit protesting together at Anaktalak Bay near Emish in August 1997. Photo: Kari Reynolds.

Innu tents set up on the blockade at Anaktalak Bay. Photo: Kari Reynolds.

Part Three: 1998–2001

Editor's Note

In the late 1990s, Tshaukuesh began leading weeks-long walks in nutshimit as a way of showing that the Innu are still using the land and to educate people about traditional ways of life. She and Francis also led canoe trips on the Mishta-shipu with similar goals. She writes lyrically about life on the land during this period and shares recipes and information about hunting and preparing food and medicine. However, the walks and canoe trips were also protests. The Mishta-shipu is central to Innu culture and history. They have paddled it and lived along it for thousands of years. The Patshishetshuanau dam, completed in 1973, had been a disaster for the Innu, as it flooded and poisoned vast areas of their land, resources, and heritage. Now a new dam on the lower part of the Mishta-shipu was being proposed. Mining and logging were ongoing and there were talks of renewed intensity of low-level flying.

NEXT PAGE:
"The lakes, the woods, the land, mosses growing everywhere, flowers . . ." Photo: Bernice Webber Penashue.

Tshaukuesh and her husband, Francis, canoeing on the Mishta-shipu. Photo: Jennifer and Kerry Saner-Harvey.

1998

February 20

L ong ago, when I was young, I used to look at the mountains in the distance with nothing but sky beyond them and long to climb to the top. I thought that was where the world ended and Heaven began.

March 8

Today Kanani, three of my grandchildren, and I drove to Patshishetshuanau to protest. My son-in-law Paul drove up in another car. As we were driving, we saw our people headed to the same place. A little while after that, we saw pineu on the road and Paul shot them for supper.

How did this happen, for Kanani to take me to the protest? She worked hard to prepare for this trip, and she drove all the way here. I knew she was tired but she pushed herself to get here safely. I wonder if she knows what this means to me and how grateful I am. It's the first time she's agreed to take me to a protest.

The timing wasn't very good, because I wanted to go to Tshenuamiu-shipu to set up our tent. They wanted me to tell stories to the Akaneshau about how the Innu used to live on the land and how I felt about the mining in Emish. Our leaders, Pone R., Peter P., and Tanien, were supposed to be there too. It was a hard decision to come, but I'm here.

March 14

When the moon first came up this evening, it was red. After a while it started to change into a brilliant ball of silver light. I felt so happy looking up at it, and I thought about what a beautiful night it was and how nice it would be to go outside for a long walk. Then I thought about the day and felt sad because we saw a lot of drunks on the road. Alcohol is a big problem in Sheshatshiu. I detest it. It's destroying us.

March 18

Today is Wednesday and it's a lovely sunny day with a nice breeze. I went outside to get firewood and hang clothes on the line. While I was doing that, enjoying the good weather, a wonderful idea came to me. We could go to nutshimit this spring on foot instead of by helicopter or bush plane! That's how our people used to travel when they went to nutshimit. It would be so wonderful if we could do it and find people to help us. I want to ask my husband what he thinks about it when he comes home from work.

May 17

My grandson Kaputshet asked me if we could go up to the mountain. I told him I couldn't leave my younger grandchildren here, but my husband suggested we take them with us. I guess he knew I needed to get outside. We started walking along the shore toward where the canoe was. As we hiked, I was worrying about two things: I was afraid the climb would be too much for the younger children, and that the flu I already had would get worse if I got too tired. Could I even make it myself? I had a bottle of water with me and I drank it as I walked and gave some to my grandchildren. We'd only gone a little way when they started getting tired. My husband said, "Maybe this is where we should stop and go back," but I refused because I was determined to reach the top of the mountain. We took it easy and we made it.

When we got to the summit I was very happy. We sat down and I took off my boots and relaxed. My husband lit a fire and made tea and we had something to eat. He and I ate fish for lunch and our grandchildren had canned food. When we'd finished our meal we stayed a while, and the children played close by.

May 20

I'm still sick, so I asked my husband if he could help me set up a little tent so I could prepare some medicine. When we'd completed the job, I told him how much his help meant to me. My son Matshen, my grandchildren, and I went off to collect boughs across the lake. When we got back with them, I spread them out on the tent floor, carefully fitting each to the next so it

Tshaukuesh helps a granddaughter load up with spruce boughs for the floor of the tent. Photo: Peter Sibbald.

Girls with ikuta in their hair. Photo: Peter Sibbald.

would be smooth. I set up the stove inside, kept my grandchildren beside me, and lit the fire. As soon as the stove was hot, I put two pots of water on to boil and put ikuta into the pots. Later that evening, when my grandchildren were asleep, I moved my bed to my little tent. It was warm and cozy inside and I lay down, stretched out my arms, and made myself comfortable on my back.

I lay there thinking about my close relatives who had died. I prayed and asked them to support me so the medicine would work. As I lay there looking up at the roof of the tent, I thought about my ancestors and how beautiful it must be wherever they are.

1999

January 3

My sister An Pinamin Pokue called me and said, "Tshaukuesh, I dreamed about you last night. I was looking for you and then we found you in the basement with a woman from Uashat. You were sewing together, making all kinds of things to earn a bit of money. You made $100 and when I saw that, I thought I'd try to find a job too." We both had a good laugh about the dream, and after I hung up I still felt happy. Her call gave me confidence.

Nin Tshaukuesh

February 23

We came to St. John's and set up two tents to show Innu life to the Akaneshau and tell them our stories. Every day a lot of people come to visit us, including schoolchildren, so it's a good opportunity to tell them about my work to protect the land, the animals, and the people. I feel that if the Akaneshau understand more about Innu life, we might get more support. I enjoy working inside the tent, making Innu doughnuts and talking to all the visitors.

A lot of people ask me how to make Innu doughnuts. I know when Akaneshau cook, they use little cups to measure, but Innu don't use them. I just put some flour and baking power into a bowl, no salt—I never use salt, even when I make bread. Flour, baking powder, raisins, molasses, brown sugar, and water—that's all. You get a big frying pan and heat it up, put some grease in it and wait until it's very hot, then put a little bit of the batter in. If the grease bubbles around it and it starts to turn brown, it's ready. Oh, I want to eat doughnuts now, just thinking about it! All my grandchildren love my doughnuts, but some people say, "Use more sugar and raisins," and others, the ones with diabetes, say, "Don't put in so much sugar and raisins." I don't know what to do!

Nin Tshaukuesh

Innu doughnuts. Photo: Chris Sampson.

March 1

This evening I called my friend Putu Ishkueu to ask her to come see me at the hotel, because I wanted to talk to her about my walk.[1] I asked her if she could find some people to come with us. I was thinking maybe people would change their minds and nobody would come. If just one person decided not to come, that might influence the others to do the same—but she says they're all coming.

I came to Natashkuan to get together with people here. I was happy at first to be visiting old friends, but I'm still afraid I might lose the walkers from Uashat and Sheshatshiu. They must be wondering where I am. They might need to reach me by phone and not be able to. Maybe I shouldn't have come.

March 18

Today we started walking. The weather isn't very good. It's snowing and the toboggans are sticking to the snow. But we headed out anyway. We crossed the Mishta-shipu and we're determined to do it. We're all very excited despite the bad weather. My son Matshen and I, my grandson Kaputshet, four women from Uashat and one man, Shinipestiss. Eight people altogether. We plodded along on our snowshoes and then stopped to make a fire and have a cup of tea and something to eat. The weather was still bad, so we didn't enjoy our meal much. Then we trekked on. My son broke the trail and the rest of us followed behind him. At one point, I saw him waiting for me and I was wondering why until I saw signs of a kak[u], tooth marks on tree bark. We might get a good meal. He called out, "Mom, let's pitch the tent here," so I said okay and we set up camp.

March 19

We're still walking and the weather is still bad. But we'll just carry on. We all got ready this morning and set out, walking very slowly in single file because we were going uphill. We made it to the top and came out of the woods onto a big marsh. After crossing two marshes, we stopped again to build a fire and then walked some more. We lost the trail for a while but found it again, and everything was okay in the end. We trekked downhill again and got to the Uapush-shipiss. As we headed down toward the river, we were all relieved to know we'd soon be setting up camp for the night.

When we got there we all worked together to pitch the tent, and then we relaxed. That's what we did today.

Nin Tshaukuesh

March 20

We're not walking today because the weather is worse. When I woke up this morning I felt happy just thinking that we were actually on the walk I so wanted to do. Then I went outside to check the weather and saw how bad it was. I wanted to talk to my friends in the other tent to decide what to do, but they were still asleep so I went back to my tent. I don't think we should walk today. We can rest here, cook, make bread for the next few days, do laundry, organize our stuff, and maybe go hunting nearby for pineu or set snares for uapush.

Nin Tshaukuesh

March 21

We stayed put yesterday and started walking again today. The weather is a little better.

March 22

The weather is very nice now—sunshine in the morning, but then in the afternoon it got warmer and the snow started to stick to our snowshoes. At noon, we made a fire and had lunch at a beautiful spot near open water. The people from Uashat had gone ahead to get things ready. When we got there, we sent the children to fetch water, but they didn't attach the bucket securely with a rope and they lost it. They tried to find it but they couldn't. We're all upset about it. After lunch, we walked again but not for long because of the soft snow. We stopped early to set up camp. Another beautiful campsite. There were signs of a kak^u nearby again, but we were so busy we didn't have time to look for it.

March 23

This morning we got up a bit late and there wasn't much bread left, as we had no time to make any last night. Anyway, we had breakfast and I said to Matshen and Kaputshet, "When we stop for tea today we'll just have bannock." The others from Uashat went on ahead of us because we weren't ready when they were, but before they left we all prayed together. After a couple of miles, Kaputshet said he was tired, so I attached his toboggan to mine and got the dog to help me pull. However, the dogs were too strong for me and they tired me out. My toes got sore from running and I got very hot and sweaty, trying to keep up with them. The snow was still soft and it was hard going. When we caught up with the people from Uashat, one of them said it looked like rain. They told me to go ahead because I'd know a good place to camp, so I took the lead with my grandson and found a nice campsite. We all worked together to set up the tent.

March 24

The sun was shining brightly this morning, and we were almost ready to leave when somebody saw a fox. The boys tried to shoot it, but they missed and it ran away. The Uashat people went on ahead again. They're very fast walkers. I was thirsty so we stopped and made a fire to make tea and have a bite to eat.

When we start walking late we don't stop at noon. We just keep going and put the tent up around two or three. Everybody is very happy when we've got the tent set up. Then the men go to get water.

March 25

We didn't leave until afternoon today. Matshen and Shinipestiss went ahead to break the trail and see which way we should go. By the time they got back, we couldn't leave because the spring sun was so warm and the snow was too soft to snowshoe on. I was discouraged and didn't know what to do with myself, but then I realized there was something I could do, so I headed for the woods to get fresh boughs for the tent floor. When I finished that task, I went for a little walk by myself, but I couldn't go far because my grandson ran after me so I turned back toward the tent.

Since we've been walking everything has gone well. No problems. We feel more confident each day: we're getting stronger and stronger. I've been wanting to do this for so long, and now it's all going well. I've seen so many beautiful things here in nutshimit.

March 26

Innut kapimutet! Innu walked here! Still in nutshimit. Today we didn't move again, because the weather is bad. The men and one woman, Putu Ishkueu, are breaking a trail and will come back this evening. I stayed in the tent with the other women, cooking and sewing.

March 27

Today we walked again, but not far. By mid-afternoon we got to a small lake and made a fire for tea and a snack. Everybody was laughing and having a good time, so I suggested we should take it easy, pitch the tent here, and relax. Soon after that, we heard a skidoo coming—my husband and my son Makkes. I gave them some tea and then they went off on the skidoo again to have a look at tomorrow's route. After they left, we waited for a while for them to come back but then decided to cross the lake on our own and set up camp before it got too dark.

March 28

Lovely weather this morning. It's time for the people from Uashat to leave us. We'll miss them so much, but it can't be helped. They have to go back to work. Before they left, I put the Innu flag out on the lake and invited them to my tent. We talked and I thanked them for all the good times. The plane landed and they headed home. A short while later my husband came back by helicopter and joined us in our tent.[2]

March 29

The snow is a bit firmer underfoot, just a bit. We got ready to go and left some stuff behind to pick up later. We started out walking on the marsh—a big marsh they call Kamassekuakamat. We all enjoyed that part of the walk, but after we got to the other side we were in dense forest so we were a bit afraid of getting lost, until somebody called out to let us know it was more open up ahead and they could see the Tshenuamiu-shipu. Then they came back to help me with my toboggan. Meanwhile, Kaputshet and Pien Jack had already found dry wood to make a fire. Shinipest said we should make the fire where we could see the sun because it would be more open there, so I found a place where you could see it nicely. I put my toboggan there too because it seemed like a good clear spot to camp. We lit the fire and made tea. I cooked some dried meat and then I dished it out for everybody.

March 30

We stayed put because it's raining. I listened to the kids talking. One of the boys, Brandon, said, "I found a good piece of wood and I want to make a bow and arrow." The other one, Tuk Pun, asked him where he found it and how big the tree was, and Brandon gestured with his hands to show him—as big around as the cooking pot! He and another boy split the branch with an axe and made the bow and arrow. I love seeing the kids doing things like that, so smart and creative! When the other boys saw them doing it, they wanted to do the same. Kaputshet started to make his own one, and Pien too. They were very happy at their task.

March 31

Here with the walking Innu in nutshimit.

We've just finished putting the tent up. The weather is terrible, snowing and very windy. This morning I didn't know what to do until Matshen said, "Let's go porcupine hunting!" and Shinipest said okay. They had just got ready to go when my husband called on the radio. I don't like talking on the radio. It makes me anxious because there's no privacy.

April 1

Once we started walking today, it stopped snowing and you could see patches of blue sky as the weather got better. This raised our spirits. Then we came out onto a small lake with a bit of open water. The young people decided to try fishing so I found a hook for them, but then they decided to wait. We walked along the shore and then stopped to discuss which way we should go next.

April 2

Today we stayed put. Matshen and Shinipest went hunting, but they didn't get anything. After they got back, Kaputshet and I put a bit of food in my bag and went out to look for animals. There was a bit of a trail so we followed it, but after a while it petered out and we had to break our own trail with snowshoes. We climbed to the top of the hill, a nice open area with a good view at the top, and had a look around, trying to see if there were any lakes nearby that we could recognize.

April 3

Innu walkers still in nutshimit. The weather is terrible and we're lost. It's the first time we've taken this route and at some point, we took a wrong turn. We can't do anything about it now because of the weather. I feel frustrated sitting around doing nothing. I wonder what the others think.

These are the people still with us on the walk to Minai-nipi:

Shinipest Rich
Tuk Pun
Pien Jack
Brandon Rich
Kaputshet, my grandson
Matshen, my son
me, Tshaukuesh

This is a story about Kaputshet, my twelve-year-old grandson. Shinipest and Matshen went hunting, looking for kak^u or pineu, but all they got was one pineu so in the afternoon Kaputshet and I went hunting. Earlier on the walk we left some food along the trail for Francis to pick up with the skidoo and bring to us, but now he can't come because of the bad weather. This is why we had to stop walking and go hunting. Not only are we lost, but we're out of food. It was snowing hard, but Kaputshet and I didn't worry about that. We took three dogs with us because the two big ones are good hunters and I wanted them to teach the little one. Also, the big ones can help me pull the toboggan.

I walked ahead to tramp down the snow with my snowshoes, but after a while Kaputshet said, "Nukum, you walk behind. I'll break the trail." It's hard work. I saw a hill and suggested we go to the top to see where we were and look for animals. He said, "Okay, Nukum," and we climbed the hill and looked around. We were hoping to see a good place for hunting, but it was difficult because of the poor visibility. I was also looking for a certain lake, hoping to recognize it, because then we wouldn't be lost anymore. I wanted to be able to go back to the camp with the good news that I knew where we were. Sometimes the snow cleared a little and I thought I could see the lake I was looking for, but I wasn't sure. We continued our trek and found another hill. We rested at the top of that one too and looked around again. We still couldn't see very well because it was snowing hard, so we went back down to try hunting again.

We continued on, and there was a lot of old man's beard in the trees. It looked so beautiful, almost as though they were decorated for Christmas. We spotted marks from where a kak^u had chewed on a tree a long time ago. I told Kaputshet that sometimes they come back again to places where they've had a good meal before. We started walking across a stream and saw where one had been chewing on a tree more recently. I looked around and heard a bird singing. We kept walking, looking for a kak^u. We separated and headed in different directions, but I started worrying that my grandson might get lost. I called out to him but he didn't answer so I turned back to look for him and called his name again. This time he answered, and we carried on but stayed closer together. Then I spotted a kak^u and called out to Kaputshet to let him know. He shot at it and said he hit it—it was still in the tree, but then I realized it was dead but stuck in the branches. I found a big long stick, so big it took two of us to get it up into the tree to pry it out, but finally it fell and we were excited to see how big it was. Kaputshet watched as I cut it open and cleaned out the insides. Then I took his photo because he was a good hunter.

He was so proud and happy. We headed back to the camp and I gave him my hunting bag so I could carry the kak^u on my back.

As we were walking back, Kaputshet said, "Nukum, don't forget you said we'd make a fire and have a cup of tea." I didn't know if we had enough time, but I didn't want to break my promise so I said, "Okay, let's do it." I laid the kak^u on the snow and Kaputshet ran to find wood for the fire. We didn't have an axe, so he broke off small branches while I looked for dry twigs and bark. He came back looking very proud with his arms full of firewood. We got a good fire going and melted snow for tea. Kaputshet got some spruce boughs and put them close to the fire for us to sit on, and we had our cups of tea and some bannock, then cleared up and headed back to the tent with the dogs, stopping to rest at one point because the kak^u was so heavy. I was hoping to find our path and retrace our steps, and in the end we did, to my relief, as I'd been afraid we'd get lost. When we got to the Uapush-shipiss, I checked to see if the ice was safe, and then showed Kaputshet the best path across. I think we might need to change our route in future when we walk to Minai-nipi, because we have to cross the river quite a few times where it winds back and forth and the ice hasn't been reliable these last few years. I was worried every time we had to cross another bend, and very relieved each time we made it to the other side and could walk on land again. Finally we made it back to the tent safely.

When they saw we had a kak^u they were very excited. They all ran over to my toboggan to have a look. "Where did you get it?" they asked, and "Who shot it?" Kaputshet asked if he could blow it up so I could scrape off the quills and clean it. I said, "Okay, go ahead." The younger children helped by getting wood and then sat around in a circle to watch. When I'd finished cleaning out the guts, I cut a stick, about three to four inches long, and sharpened it so I could sew up the belly. I left a short piece of intestine near the anus for Kaputshet to blow into. Once the kak^u was inflated, I went outside by the lake and made a fire to burn off the quills, and then I used a sharp knife to scrape the skin all over. You have to make sure all the quills are burned off because they're very sharp. When I finished scraping, I took it into the tent again to cut it up. The children followed me to watch what I was doing. I put my pot on the stove and they all asked how long it would take to cook. "Maybe an hour or two," I said. "If you cook it too fast it will be tough, and I want it to be tender." When it was ready, I served the meat and put oatmeal in the broth to thicken it for soup and we had a feast.

Sometimes you can see signs that porcupines are around. You can see their tracks in the snow, or the marks where they were chewing on the bark of trees. If you just see marks on one or two trees, it probably isn't around, though—you need to see them on a lot of trees and then you know it's probably nearby. Sometimes you'll see one in a tree, and if you have a gun you can shoot it, or if you have an axe you can chop the tree down if it's small enough and then hit the porcupine with the axe. Either way, you have to be careful to hit it on the head, not the stomach, because if you damage the stomach, it'll be much harder to clean and sew up. When you finish singeing it in the fire, you have to wash it, or in the winter you can just put it under the snow and roll it around to clean it, and then you scrape it with a knife. But in the summer, you have to clean it in the water. Then you cut it up and cook it.

I usually cook porcupine in a big cooking pot. The cooking time depends on how big it is, maybe two hours. When it's cooked, you take the meat out of the pot and put the broth back on the stove to make soup. You add some mashkushiu-nushkuauat—oatmeal—or some macaroni, and some salt, and stir it with a big spoon for a few minutes, and then you serve it to everybody with the meat. It's delicious! The kids love it and sometimes, if there's any left over, I reheat it and have it for a bedtime snack. When all the meat is gone, we can have the soup for another meal. It's so good!

April 4

We've been waiting a few days now for a helicopter to pick us up and take us home. Some of the young people think we should walk home, but I think we'll be too weak because we don't have enough food. Also, a lot more snow has fallen now and we'd have to break a new trail all the way. They started arguing about who would have to break the trail, which made me feel sad. I think it would be better to take a different route home if we have to walk back, but there's a lot of fresh deep snow whichever way we go.

Finally, I said to them: "How are we going to walk all the way back? We're hungry. There's no food. We need to be strong to walk. Apart from that, even if we go back the way we came, we won't find our old campsites because they'll be buried under the snow, so we'll have to start from scratch and cut new tent poles every night." I guess they're thinking it would be easy to walk back, because they're young and don't have much experience. I had to work hard to get people to come on the first walk.

Some people told me, "Tshaukuesh, I can't walk with you, I smoke too much," or "I've got high blood pressure," or "I've got diabetes." Others said, "I've never, ever walked so far in my life," or "I can't do it because I'm overweight." I didn't argue. I just kept bringing it up every day, hoping to persuade them bit by bit. And then when we actually did the walk last year, we had to turn back. They said, "Tshaukuesh, I just can't do it." I didn't want to give up before we got to Minai-nipi but I couldn't do it all by myself.

This year the weather has been terrible. Right now, it's snowing so hard we can't see anything. We're still hoping the helicopter might come this evening. We have no food, nothing. All our supplies are used up. I feel very, very sad that we didn't quite make it and I don't have anything to cook for the kids. I went onto the beach to look for pineu and I managed to get two of them, but I really needed three to feed everybody properly. I would have got more, only the dogs barked and scared them away.

I feel so angry at the utshimau, the Innu Nation and the band council. Why don't they support the walk? Why don't they look after the people in nutshimit? It's very, very important, this walk I'm doing—I don't want the Akaneshau to say we don't need our land, so they can take it over. We need to show them we're using it. If I was on the band council I'd support this work we're doing.

When I walk in nutshimit with my people, I'm showing how much we respect Innu culture, the natural world, and all living things. I want people to know we won't give up our land. We won't allow the government to damage it with mines and dams and bombs. If I was elected to the Innu Nation or the band council, I'd put all my energy into this and I'd look after the people walking in nutshimit.

Every time I leave nutshimit, I try to find some special way to let the land know that I'll be back. I say goodbye to the plants, the animals, even the tent poles we leave behind. Today I went down to the beach and found a crooked tree. I hugged it and said: "I'm leaving but I'll come back. Don't be sad." I started crying, still hugging the tree. And then I walked on, looking for pineu.

"Innut kapimutet! Innu walked here!" Photo: Penashue family collection.

"I used a sharp knife to scrape the skin all over." Photo: Jennifer and Kerry Saner-Harvey.

April 5

The helicopter finally came and got us. While we were in the air I looked out the window to see where we had walked. I felt very proud we'd come so far—we almost made it this time. But I also cried because I wished that I was still walking down there, surrounded by lakes and rivers, trees, mountains, the animals. So beautiful.

Nin Tshaukuesh

April 10

Today I was thinking about how I hadn't walked on our land for so many years, but all those years I was thinking, "I want to go, I want to go. I want to walk where my ancestors walked, where I walked with my parents when I was young." I can see my mom and dad, my brothers and my sisters, all of us so happy, walking in nutshimit. When my father found a good hunting place with plenty of animals, we'd stop and camp for a couple of months. And then we'd move on.

We were hunters. I have so many memories of those years and I've wanted to walk again for so long, but there were too many challenges. Now I'm so glad I didn't give up on the idea.

Letter to the women of Uashat:

Thank you so much for walking with me. The only place I found anyone to support me this year was Uashat. I want to tell you how happy you made me when you came on the walk with me. Nobody complained or argued, we got along so well. We always found something to laugh about and we always worked together cheerfully. We shared everything, the Quebec people and the Sheshatshiu people—we ate together and we thanked each other for sharing. I'm very grateful to you and I'll never forget you. This was a demonstration of our determination to protect our land and our culture for our children and future generations. This is Innu land. We showed the government and the people how much it means to us—Nitassinan, our homeland. When the elders are gone, our children and grandchildren will use it. The women were an example for others when we led the protests, and our walk will also inspire people. Sometimes people talk about what should be done, but they don't do it. We didn't just talk about it; we did it.

Everything went well even though we did have some problems. First we wasted time going in the wrong direction, and then we got lost. Some people said maybe we should give up, but I reminded them that even if we couldn't finish, even if we never made it to Minai-nipi, this walk would still be a huge accomplishment.

This is my second walk, and now I know what we need to do to succeed next time. We need a guide, a leader to show us the best meshkanau. I don't know how to use a map, but once I've walked the route two or three times, especially if somebody can show me the way, then I'll know. I'm so happy that I know what to do next year now, so glad we didn't give up. One more trip and I'll never get lost again.

Thank you.

April 19

I dreamed about my old boyfriend last night. Why did I dream that? I wasn't thinking about him before I went to sleep. Matthew Rich. His Innu name is Mantush, the Innu word for "insect." I dreamed we were at Kakatshu-utshistun, Raven's Nest, just the two of us walking on the ice along the shore, arm in arm, kissing each other, hugging and cuddling, laughing together. He was holding me close, and I was wondering what it was leading up to. I felt lighthearted and joyful, filled to the brim with love and happiness. In my dream I thought, "Oh, this is the first time anybody ever loved me this much." We walked almost halfway round Kakatshu-utshistun, kissing and hugging all the way, me and Mantush. Then we got to my parents' tent on the shore. I walked into the tent, feeling apprehensive. I saw the teapot on the stove, so I poured tea into cups and handed one to Mantush. He took it and stood in the doorway. I drank my tea and then I realized my mom was okay, not angry or upset. The inside of the tent was really nice, and that's all I remember of the dream. I wonder why I had that dream—I was thinking about something completely different when I went to sleep.

Nin Tshaukuesh

May 29

In nutshimit. Sometimes there's a bit of a problem when I go to nutshimit. My grandchildren want to come and I hate to say no to them because I know how much they love it, but then when I get there and set up camp, I realize I've brought too many of them and I can't look after all of them properly. I have so much work to do and I need some time to myself, but I have so much responsibility. No adults to help me. I always used to write my journal in nutshimit, but now I don't have any free time. I can only write a little bit.

June 1

It's raining. My grandson Kaputshet wanted to go hunting in the afternoon before the weather got even worse. He went down to the beach. When I saw him getting ready to go, I said, "Be careful! An eagle might get you!" "Why did you say that?" he asked. "Don't you know how much I love to go walking and hunting?" I was so surprised and happy to hear him say that. I thought it was very clever of him at such a young age.

Nin Tshaukuesh

August 9

I flew here to Ottawa with an Akaneshau woman. I'm a little confused because I thought this meeting was only for Indigenous women and I was looking forward to that, but then I saw there were two Akaneshau women from Goose Bay in our group, along with Nympha Byrne and me. The Akaneshau women invited us and they paid for everything, but I don't understand why. It's a big meeting, and they were invited by the organizers but we weren't. I wondered why they didn't send invitations to us Innu women. After I explained how I felt to one of the organizers, she seemed surprised and said that she thought we were all Innu. The meeting started again and someone passed us a note. When the Akaneshau women saw it they started whispering to each other. I don't know what they said, but the note said that the conference organizer wanted to talk to the four of us. I think she asked them if they were Innu or Metis,[3] but I'm not sure. Then she asked me if I wanted to say something so I did, with Nympha translating. I said I never knew these people were Innu, I thought they were Akaneshau, but I guess they're Metis. The two women didn't look happy with me. When we went back to the meeting, I asked why they didn't send an invitation to us Innu women. I tried not to get upset, but

I wanted to share my confusion about what had happened. After that, they never invited us again.

It's very troubling.

Nin Tshaukuesh

August 10

I'm writing on the plane because when I get back to Sheshatshiu I won't have time. I'm trying to figure out why the Innu women have stopped speaking out and fighting the government. I think this is why: we were waiting for somebody to take the initiative and decide what to do next, but nobody did and then it seemed too late; people were apathetic and lost their focus. That's what I think. I don't know what the other women think. When we were more politically active, many of us had fewer children and grandchildren, less housework and cooking. I myself had fewer grandchildren, and some of them lived in Uashat so I didn't have to look after them. Now they're all in Sheshatshiu. Some of the younger women didn't have any children then, and they helped the rest of us too. Also, at the beginning of the protests, most Innu women didn't care so much about working for money. They cared more about protecting the land and the animals, but now more women want jobs and money.

Nin Tshaukuesh

August (undated)

This morning my sister An Pinamin Pokue called me on the phone. She said, "Tshaukuesh, we're going to the marsh to get some bakeapples. Would you like to come?" I said, "Maybe, we'll see." After I hung up I thought about it. I'm so busy but I didn't want to say no, so I called them and said, "Okay, I'm coming." In the afternoon, we left for Matshiteu. We walked and walked, looking for bakeapples. I wanted to try a new place so I started walking along the edge of the marsh until my sister called me, wondering where I was, and then I went back to her. There used to be lots of bakeapples when we were younger, but this year we hardly found any, which made me sad. We made a fire and had a cup of tea, then we went home.

It was a nice walk but we didn't get many bakeapples.

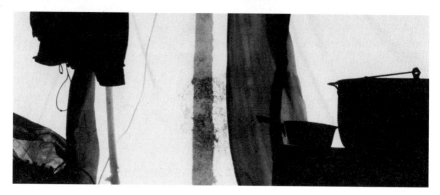

September 3, Uashat

I came here by train from Uapush for a kids' hockey tournament. I always want to stop and get out, but you can't until the train gets to the station. I'd really prefer to walk so my feet could feel the earth, the marsh, the caribou moss. It doesn't feel the same in a vehicle; you go past things so fast, you can't touch them and you miss all the nice places. When Francis and I walk along the road, he walks on the pavement but I never do. When you walk in the woods you can see where to set your feet, and I love the physical feeling of putting my foot in just the right place. And you can decide for yourself where you want to stop and rest. Sometimes I don't just sit down, I lie right down on the ground. When you do that you can feel the earth with your whole body and you can think more clearly. I look up at the sky and sometimes I pray, surrounded by the animals who protect us. When I was born my parents laid me on the ground in the tent; no bed, just right on the ground.

September 4

I just got home last night and I'm exhausted, but I have to cook Innu pancakes for breakfast. Makkes called and said, "We should go to nutshimit." I asked him how long he wanted to stay there and he said, "Until just before Christmas." I said I'd think about it. Later on, Peter came over and said, "We should go to nutshimit." I started to laugh and I said, "How did you come up with the same idea as Makkes? He called this morning and said the same thing." I decided to talk to Francis and maybe go with Makkes. We couldn't go with both, because they wanted to go in different directions.

September 20

I had a dream. Mani-Katinen Nuna and I were walking in the hills through the forest. When I looked down, I realized I was close to the edge of a high cliff and I was afraid of falling. Then we did fall, but we somehow managed to scramble back up by clinging to a fallen tree. Then we started walking again in a beautiful area, and after a while we came to a tent belonging to an Akaneshau the Innu call Misk Utshimau. He hadn't set it up right, not the Innu way—the poles were all crooked. I kept thinking about the dream,

Francis canoeing on the Mishta-shipu. Photo: Jennifer and Kerry Saner-Harvey.

Bakeapples. Photo: Sander Meurs.

Shadows on tent wall with cooking pots. Photo: Navarana Igloliorte.

trying to analyze it. I think the message was not to blame myself if something bad happened because I wasn't strong enough to prevent it, not to be sad or afraid but to move forward and try my best to succeed, even if it's very difficult. That's my interpretation of my dream.

Nin Tshaukuesh

September 21

We call this place Mishtushashk^u. My husband and I and some of our children are here, eight of us altogether. This is the first time I remember that the band council didn't pay for the plane. Francis and Peter paid. I was very happy when the plane landed. I helped to unload everything and then I went on to the beach—so good to be here! As I walked along the shore, I picked some alder twigs and held them in my hands while I said a prayer of gratitude for the beauty all around us.

In the evening, I set up the radio and my son and grandson went with Francis to put a fishing net in the water. When they came back, they brought two ducks. It was getting dark and I didn't have time to clean them, so I said I'd do it the next day. We made some toast because I was too tired to make a proper supper.

September 22

After breakfast, my husband went to check the nets with two of our grandchildren, Kaputshet and Thea. They came back with four trout, which I cleaned and cooked. As we were eating them, I was thinking about how when men go hunting in nutshimit and bring back fish or meat, the women always start cleaning it right away. The reason for this is that it shows respect for the animals. The animal spirits know the hunters are looking for them, but they understand we need to eat and so they give us something as long as we respect them. That's how we Innu do it in nutshimit—how we've always done it.

Nin Tshaukuesh

September 25

Still here in nutshimit. When I finished all the work in the tent, we went out in two canoes: my husband, Pineshish, Kaputshet, and me in one; Peter and three of his children, Jean Paul, Ben, and Thea in the other. We paddled until we came to a paustik^u, and then Peter and Francis took the canoes through the rapids while the rest of us walked. Then we all got back in the canoes and paddled until we came to another big paustik^u, where my grandchildren and I got out again. They saw some ducks and were dying to go into the rapids to get them but I said, "No, it's too dangerous." Instead, I took them across the lake where I'd seen a fishing camp. We stopped there to have a look and then they wanted to explore further, but the route was too difficult so we hiked to a different lake where we waited for my husband and Peter. They didn't come for a long time, so I started to worry and said to the children, "Maybe your dad and grandfather are looking for us." Finally, they arrived and explained that they'd been looking for a net we lost a couple of days ago. They still hadn't found it, so they went off again and I stayed on the beach with my grandchildren. I was still worried, afraid they might have an accident, but there was nothing I could do so I started praying for them. Then my grandchildren called out to say they were coming and Peter shouted to me, asking if I wanted to get back in the canoe again or walk. He said Francis had gone ahead to find a nice sandy place for us to stop. I had cut some boughs and I said I'd walk, but I gave him the boughs to take in the canoe. Then my grandchildren and I walked on until we saw where they were waiting for us. They had lots of fish because they'd found the net full of salmon and trout, and then we found a good spot, cut more boughs to sit on, and cleaned the fish. Lots of fish to clean!

September 26

We're still here at Mishtushashk^u. It's Sunday, beautiful weather. This morning while we were checking the snares we collected some long, smooth, dry sticks to make a frame for hanging caribou meat to dry over a fire. Then my husband butchered the caribou we had in the tent. Once the meat is dry, you don't have to worry about the flies getting into it.

September 27

Some of us wanted to stay here and some wanted to go into the mountains. In the end, after much discussion, we all decided to go. We paddled along the shore in the two canoes, and when we got close to the mountains, we went ashore to start walking. After a while we came to a brook, not very wide but deep, so we stopped to figure out how to get across. Peter and Francis cut down two trees to make a narrow bridge and we all crossed, first the children, then me, using poles so we wouldn't lose our balance. I was laughing as I crossed because I was afraid I'd fall and get soaked—very relieved to get to the other side. The scenery around us was so beautiful, and after a while we sat down to rest and enjoy it—we could see a long way into the distance. The kids looked so happy and so was I.

When we got to the top of the mountain I saw that Kaputshet was missing, and one of the boys told me he'd stayed behind looking for pineu and was waiting for someone to bring him a gun. One of the men went back to take him one and once they got a pineu they came back. Kaputshet loves hunting so much.

Nin Tshaukuesh

September 29

Still in nutshimit. This morning Peter and Ben got ready to go caribou hunting with Francis. They took a canoe and I stayed in the tent with Pineshish and three of the grandchildren. After they left I started working. I made a fire for the caribou meat and then I did some cooking and laundry. It's so beautiful out today and I love being here with my family, all together.

Nin Tshaukuesh

September 30

Two of my grandchildren and I walked back to get the canoe we left behind yesterday. After we got it, we paddled across a small pond and as we were crossing we saw a lot of pineu flying overhead. We were all very excited—the grandchildren kept shouting "Another one! And another one!" After we landed the canoe, we followed them into the woods and Francis shot several. I plucked them and then we went out in the canoe again, stopping to walk around some rapids, then paddling back along the shore to the tent. During the portage, Francis carried the canoe on his head, Kaputshet took the paddles, and Thea and I took the rest of the equipment on our backs. When we got home to the tent we were all very pleased to have made it back with plenty to eat. I cooked the pineu for supper and it was delicious.

Nin Tshaukuesh

October 1

Waiting for the plane to go back to Sheshatshiu.

November 5

I've had enough! There are so many obstacles and barriers. I don't seem to have any results to show for all the work I've done. I'm trying to keep our land from being destroyed. I'm not wasting time or doing something wrong; I'm right and this is very important. I'm going to persevere, not for money but as an activist who is deeply committed to protecting the land and the animals before it's too late.

Nin Tshaukuesh

November 16

Peter won the election![4] A lot of people supported him and they're all thrilled. I hope he works very hard for the Innu of Natuashish and Sheshatshiu and does a good job. I hope he doesn't forget the land.

Nin Tshaukuesh

December 5

Open letter to the women outside Nitassinan:

My friends, I'm very sorry you haven't heard from us lately. Now I'll tell you what happened. It's hard to explain what I have to say, how I feel. I'm an Innu woman. I'm still on the move, in good health and active. I'm not a very old lady yet. My life is still dedicated to protecting the land. Even though you haven't heard from us lately, we haven't given up. You may have heard last year that I was walking on the land with four women and a man from Uashat, and some people from Sheshatshiu. We go to nutshimit every year. Everything we do is to protect the land: protesting, speaking, or walking—it's all part of it. In nutshimit we teach the young people our culture and we live a healthy life. We aren't in the media so much as before, when you used to hear us speaking out. I know you don't see the women protesting and going to jail anymore. It's not the same now but we haven't given up; we're still trying to protect our land.

Thank you so much for your support. I'm sorry I didn't send you our news sooner, but I feel better now that I've let you know what's happening with us.

Nin Tshaukuesh

2000

January 2

I'm at Matshiteu in Ishkueu's cabin with three of my grandchildren and an Akaneshau woman. It's very cold here and there isn't enough firewood so we'll have to look for more. I'll tell you why I came here: to have a rest. I'm hoping to have a good sleep tonight. I'm so tired after working so hard all December to get ready for Christmas and New Year, so I decided to come here to regain my strength. I hope it works!

Nin Tshaukuesh

January 11

Today we went to a women's meeting about our concerns for the land and our children's future—three Innu women and two Akaneshau. It was a good meeting, and we decided to try to keep meeting regularly.

January 18

Another good women's meeting this evening in Sheshatshiu—six Innu women and two Akaneshau women. We talked about how we feel lost and confused, without direction. We talked about the government and about local women's issues and what we should do next. The women are concerned about so many things that are happening in Sheshatshiu. It would be good to keep getting together regularly. We're very strong women; if we sit down together and listen to each other we always come up with good ideas and find a way forward. That's what I think.

Nin Tshaukuesh

January 22

I'm going to talk about what I've been doing and thinking. Last Saturday afternoon I went to my tent at Nishuasht Kaitashtet with my grandson Nikashantess and an Akaneshau woman. Here's what we did:first, we beat

Tshaukuesh on the Mishta-shipu. Photo: Penashue family collection.

down a path through the snow with our snowshoes, then we made a fire, then we went and got water to make tea and had something to eat. After that, Nikashantess and I went outside and beat down some more snow on a hill so it would harden overnight for my grandchildren to slide on tomorrow. Then I went back and forth along the path, cutting lots of boughs and taking them back to the tent bit by bit. That's what I did. It's very cold outside and I'm quite worried because I have a sore throat and laryngitis, and I'm afraid I might be making it worse. But I can't help it, I love working outdoors!

Nin Tshaukuesh

January 23

When I woke up this morning I was wondering what to do. I wanted to go along the road to get boughs for the tent floor, so I called Ishkueu and asked her if she was going to Goose Bay. She said yes, so I took a ride with them and got out on the road, just me and my dog. Then I started to cut the boughs. I'm only worried about one thing: I still have a sore throat and I don't want to make it worse. It's extremely cold out. However, when it was time to go home I was very happy to have the boughs.

Nin Tshaukuesh

February 3

This is a letter to family members who have died:

Dear people,

I want to ask your advice. You see me and you know what I'm doing. I don't want to give up protecting our culture, our land, our people, and the generations to come. But it's daunting. I feel overwhelmed and I cry when I think about it. There are so many issues. It's hard to find allies and I feel alone, but I need to be strong. We have problems at home too. What should I do? Please tell me. I wish you could give me an answer tonight!

Nin Tshaukuesh

February 3

I'm writing this on the plane to Goose Bay from Natuashish. We went to a funeral for an old lady named Mineskuess. A lot of people from Natuashish and Sheshatshiu were there. It was so sad—a lot of people crying. She had a lot of children, grandchildren, and great-grandchildren. There were many moving eulogies for her, telling the stories of her life. Her granddaughter gave an especially touching one about how much she loved and misses her. Two people from Sheshatshiu spoke too—Peter and me. I was glad we made it to the funeral to pray for our grandmother and to say goodbye.

Nin Tshaukuesh

March 14

We've just started out on the spring walk. The weather isn't very good. It's been hard work pulling the toboggans and the dogs can't help much because there's too much snow.

We decided to set up camp after walking just a short distance. It's getting dark and they're still putting the tent up. The younger boys went to get firewood—Kaputshet and Tony Penashue Jr.—but it isn't very good wood, probably because they couldn't see in the dark. We finally got the fire burning weakly and everybody was tired so we got ready for bed. The end of the first day.

Nin Tshaukuesh

March 15

This morning we crossed the Mishta-shipu, the young people in the lead and the elders behind. Rose Pokue has a toboggan and is walking with a young boy. After we crossed the river we walked along the shore. I was using a small komatik, not a toboggan, with the dogs helping me pull. When I walk with a komatik I have a hard time with my dogs at first, but then they get trained after a few days. The young people walked ahead for a while and then stopped to wait for us. I asked them if they could take my sled with the dogs so I could go ahead, because the dogs work harder if I'm in front of them. Rose and I walked ahead, proud to be breaking the trail and happy to be walking, even though we were very tired. I felt like singing so I sang, "I walk on my own two feet to protect the land. I never give up." I was afraid they'd hear me singing and laugh at me, so I didn't sing too loud.

Today was a struggle and we got lost, because there was so much snow we couldn't tell which way to go. Eventually we heard help coming in the form of a skidoo. They took two of the young men and the tent and stove so they could go ahead and start setting up the camp. Then they came back again and took us to where the young men were, camped very close to the trail, on the other side of the marsh. The next day the people with the skidoo came back and took all our gear and the small children. The rest of us walked. By the time we got to the campsite they had already cut poles and collected some boughs for the floor. They were still hard at work, though, so we all pitched in to help them. Once we got the tent set up, the boys went hunting, my grandson Kaputshet and Tony Penashue. They'd seen where a kak[u] had been eating bark, so they went back that way to look for it. After a little while I heard a shot and then they came back with the kak[u]. I cleaned and cooked it and then we ate supper, all very happy. We stayed there two days, Friday and Saturday, and started walking again on Sunday. We rested until then because the weather was so bad.

March 19

Francis came with the skidoo. The weather was terrible and the young people started saying we should give up and go back to Sheshatshiu. I was very sad when I heard that. Francis was going to head back, but he decided to stay another night because we needed help and he was tired. Pineshish and his girlfriend are staying too, until the 21st, and then Francis will be back on March 22 with Tuminik Pokue and my sister with one of her grandsons.

We camped by a small stream. The boys are still saying they want to go back to Sheshatshiu.

March 23

This morning Francis went back to Sheshatshiu with the kids who wanted to leave. Tuminik stayed with his wife and one grandson. Then we started to walk. We walked a very long way today.

March 25

Started walking again, to Tshenuamiu-shipu. Before stopping for the night, we made a fire and had tea. After we got to the camp the boys killed another kak^u. Then Pineshish and his girlfriend went back to Sheshatshiu, and I sent one kak^u back with them. I tried to convince him to stay but he really wanted to go, though he said he'd come back later. After he left with the skidoo I went for a walk by myself, on snowshoes with my dogs, along the trail. After a while I sat down and prayed for my son and I cried. I asked the Creator to help me because I felt so sad that everybody wanted to go home.

Now we have to walk without skidoo support, because the snow and ice are melting and the skidoos can't get through. We started to walk—me, my sister An Pinamin, her daughter, Kaputshet, and my grandson, and my sister's five-year-old grandson. When we stopped to set up the tent the weather was bad, mixed snow and rain, very mushy snow for a tent base. Next day we walked again to An-mani Ushakaikan.

March 29

We walked again today, just across the lake, and then we stopped because there was open water and we wanted to go fishing.

Tshaukuesh and Ishkueu. Photo: Penashue family collection.

March 30
Still walking.

March 31
Bad weather, soft snow. I can't write much in my journal because I'm so tired and we don't have much to eat. Everybody is exhausted.

April 1
This morning my husband told me on the radio that the weather is really bad. He said he'd call again this afternoon. I said we're going to walk today, but not very far. We're almost at Minai-nipi. We'll wait there for the plane to take us out again.

April 2
Back in Sheshatshiu. The bush plane took three people in the first load and my sister and I stayed to take the tent down and get everything packed up. We made it to Minai-nipi! We made it, we made it! No skidoos, just walking on our own feet. I'm so glad we persevered—we never gave up, even when we were exhausted we kept on walking. I'll miss the walk!

April 19, Utshimassit
I'm writing on the plane. I had trouble getting a seat, but finally I got one and I feel so relieved. I wanted to come to this meeting so badly because I want to speak about protecting the land. It's a meeting about the Mishta-shipu—they want to build another dam.[5] At first, I didn't see any Innu at the airport, only Akaneshau, and I thought maybe they had already left, but then an Akaneshau woman came and asked, "Do you people want to go to Davis Inlet?" She said she'd take me to where the plane was. When we got there, I saw Innu people—Simon Michel and Nancy Nuna—and I was very happy. Sometimes if you persevere, all of a sudden, your problems are solved. I love it when that happens.
    Nin Tshaukuesh

Francis with a komatik. Photo: Jennifer and Kerry Saner-Harvey.

May 6

Today we came to nutshimit. Two pontoon planes brought all our stuff out here. Then a helicopter brought Mani-Katinen and me and the children—one of my granddaughters, Pishum, and one of Mani-Katinen's grandchildren. I loved seeing the land spread out beneath us as we flew and knowing we were going there. I'm not afraid of flying in a helicopter, but I was afraid the military jets might hit us because there's a lot of low-level flying in the spring. I told the pilot I was scared and he pointed to some jets in the distance.

I looked below us, trying to see where we walked last spring, to see our meshkanau. I could see Minai-nipi where we walked when it was frozen. Then I saw a tamarack forest that I call "My Father's Woods," because my dad once told me that a tamarack tree had talked to him and asked him if he had daughters. He said yes, lots of daughters, and the tree said to send them out to cut wood. That was his way of encouraging us not to be lazy.

We saw more tamarack, and then I saw An-mani Ushakaikan and Tshaukuesh Minishtikuss and the place where we camped when we walked this way last month. I thought about how strong we were to walk all that way and I felt very proud that we made it.

Now we're here at Minai-nipi; we've landed on the beach and set up camp. In the evening when we finished our work I decided to try to find some Innu medicine, ikuta, to boil on the stove. When I smell the steam, I know it's good medicine, very soothing and restoring. Then I broke a caribou bone and ate the pimi. Every time I come to nutshimit I always take this medicine, ikuta and pimi. In Sheshatshiu I often feel tired and ill, and I need to do this to get my strength back. Another thing that's very healing is to experience the beauty of the land, the lakes, the trees, the sounds of the animals, the fresh food. I feel so happy to be here with my children and grandchildren.

Nin Tshaukuesh

May 7

When I woke up this morning I felt like a new woman. I think last night's medicine helped. I got up and made a fire in the stove, then I lay down again to wait until it got going, and then I got up again to make breakfast. After we ate, I told my grandchildren we were going to go into the woods to get more boughs for the tent floor. We walked on the beach and the first boughs looked strange, as if they'd been scorched, but then we found some better ones. I was disturbed to see the scorched boughs, though, and I thought maybe it was caused by low-level flying.

May 16

I got up at five this morning and made the fire. Then I went to Matshen's tent and made a fire there too. After breakfast, his girlfriend and I walked along a beautiful section of shoreline looking for boughs, which I put in an uiushun and left there for Matshen to pick up with the skidoo.

In the evening, the snow was mushy and the tents were all crooked, so we moved Matshen's to a new place and got it set up nice and straight, with fresh-packed snow for a base. Since Matshen is the only man here and there are two tents to move, we did one today and we'll move the other one tomorrow. We're all going to stay together tonight in the one tent. That's what I did today.

Nin Tshaukuesh

May 20

Still at Minai-nipi. The birds woke me up this morning. It's wonderful to hear them singing so I stayed still and listened for a while, thinking about how I was hearing the same bird calls I heard as a child. I got up and made the fire and then lay down again, but I had the impression that the birds were trying to persuade me to get up. Then after a while they moved away, as if one of them had said, "Okay, Tshaukuesh is awake now." Then I thought about another kind of bird, a kautauassikunishkueunishit, which Innu people used to say had a call that said, "Tante nipatshi nita kutshikutshin?"—"How can I dive down and come back up?" I hadn't heard that bird for a long time. I wonder where they've all gone. Then I got up in a nice warm tent.

Nin Tshaukuesh

May 25

We haven't seen the sun this morning. When I went outside I saw Utshesh Nuna, Mani-Katinen's husband, coming toward us along the shore where I'd put up my clothesline. He told us he'd seen a kak^u in a tree nearby, which was very surprising, so close to the tent. Kaputshet got his gun and some ammunition and went out to try to shoot it. I went out with my camera to get

a picture of him hunting. I was happy to see him so excited and full of energy, and I felt proud that he was a good hunter. When he brought it to me, I told him I'd check my snares first and then clean the kak^u, and I asked Matshiu if he wanted to come with me. The first snare was empty so I told him to put one of his snares there to see if he'd have better luck. I didn't have any uapush, so we got some wood to make a fire to cook the kak^u. Then I cleaned the kak^u in a nice tidy place. I don't like to prepare food unless everything is clean and neat.

In the afternoon, the weather was bad and we were almost out of wood, so I asked Kaputshet to go and split some more. He was reluctant at first but in the end, he went. I called him back when I thought he had enough, but then he said he wanted to keep going. I was a bit afraid he might cut himself. When he finally came back I asked him to bring some wood into the tent, but again he was reluctant so I started getting ready to go and get it myself. Then he repented and said he'd go after all so I wouldn't have to get wet. I said, "Thanks for that, Kaputshet! I'll sleep well tonight!" I love it when my children and grandchildren say kind things to each other and to me—these are the things I long to hear.

Nin Tshaukuesh

May 30

This afternoon, Matshen got back from beaver hunting with two other people. They hadn't got any and Matshen was injured. We tried to help but we couldn't, so we called a doctor, but he said he couldn't come and he'd send an airlift instead. In the end, a helicopter came around two to take Matshen to the hospital with his girlfriend and daughter. After they left, Francis and I went out on the water with two of our grandchildren and Utshesh and Mani-Katinen. It was a lovely sunny day and we enjoyed ourselves. We saw some goose and ducks, but unfortunately, we didn't have the right ammunition. Kaputshet tried with the .22 but he couldn't get them, to his great disappointment. I felt sad when I saw his downcast face. We continued

Tent interior. Photo: Navarana Igloliorte.

The kautuasikunestkuenest. Photo: Ingrid Taylar.

"Then I got up in a nice warm tent." Photo: Penashue family collection.

on our way, looking for a good spot to have a boil-up. I made some tea and cooked some fish and then we ate together.

Nin Tshaukuesh

June 4

It rained in the night and I was afraid everything we'd left outside would be soaked. I got up and made a fire, then went outside to see. I wish I'd had time last night to organize my things and put a tarp over them! I was so busy before I went to bed. I took one of my bags inside the tent and everything in it was wet. I washed my face and made tea and coffee, then I strung a clothesline up inside the tent and hung my things up to dry. After that I went to get water and started to think about breakfast.

I thought fish would be good, so I decided to go out and get the ones Matshen had caught in his net yesterday and left to chill under the snow. I picked some of the best ones, trout, cleaned them and brought them inside. I decided to cook them the way my mother used to, boiled with a bit of salt. When they were ready I thickened the broth with flour and made some bannock. The older people ate the fish but the little ones just wanted corn flakes. After breakfast, I tidied the tent and Mani-Katinen and I went out in the canoe to our last campsite to get the axe we'd left behind. When we got there, we collected all our old tent poles and stood them up together so they wouldn't rot. Afterward we tidied everything up and burned the garbage, then paddled further along the shore to retrieve some snowshoes I'd left there. After that we went back to the tent and put the snowshoes and axe away. Next, I cooked supper, did the dishes after we ate, and then made a cake for Kaputshet's birthday. While it cooled I made icing. Kaputshet was delighted about the birthday party and cake.

Nin Tshaukuesh

July 7

I'm in St. John's to visit Kanani and the children. I've had a headache since I got here and I feel shivery, maybe because I was so tired when I left home, and then on Saturday morning we went to the opening of the Beothuk archeological site at Boyd's Cove, where we'd been invited to speak.

Francis cleaning a caribou leg bone prior to breaking it to get pimi. Photo: Jennifer and Kerry Saner-Harvey.

Long ago, the Akaneshau killed the Beothuk because they hated Indigenous people so much. They despised them, so they murdered them. There were a lot of people at the site and many made speeches. Everybody was reading the storyboards that explained what happened, and I was glad Peter was there to translate them for me. After that, we walked to where the Beothuk used to live, a very nice place. We saw a statue somebody had made of an Innu woman.[6] It's very beautiful, and so is the spot where she's standing. Then we walked further and found an old campsite. You could see where they had their tents; it looked like nutshimit, surrounded by trees with green moss covering the ground. Afterward, we Innu from Sheshatshiu talked for a long time about these long-ago Innu. They were rejected and hated, the ones that were abused.

July 10

Sometimes I wish I could just be in a quiet place so I could concentrate and write my journal. Occasionally that does happen, but never for long enough. When I have had the chance to be in such a place, my mind is so clear I can really focus. Sometimes I have things to say that are very important and I need to write them down so I don't forget.

Everything's okay here and I've been getting lots of rest. Only one thing: when I look at Kanani, my heart goes out to her because she works so hard trying to get an education and bring the children up on her own. It hurts me when I see how alone she is, struggling so hard. I know how much she loves her children. She tries so hard to take good care of them and make them happy. She never gives up, even if she's having a hard time; her work is endless.

Nin Tshaukuesh

July 12

I'm still in St. John's, still trying to find a quiet place here—where can I find one? I try to get up early in the morning before everybody else, before the noise starts; I have breakfast and wash and get everything ready, then I sit down at the table to write. This makes me happy—it's so peaceful, everybody asleep. But then, just as I get started, they start getting up. It gets noisy and I can't think straight. I wish I could find a place where I could have at least a couple of hours of quiet. I'll keep trying to find somewhere.

December 5

I'm on a plane on my way to Montreal with Manteskueu to attend a book launch.[7] They want me to speak and I can talk about whatever I want: animals, Nitassinan, the environment, Innu pakasiun, Innu-aitun ...

December 7

Still in Montreal, leaving for Toronto next. I'm going to speak in Toronto and then fly to St. John's for one night on Sunday, then back to Goose Bay the next day and on to Sheshatshiu. I've been to many places since leaving home, working too hard, no time for a rest. Don't people realize I'm tired? I'm starting to get homesick. I miss my family. I hope the rest of the trip will be okay.

Nin Tshaukuesh

December 10

It's Sunday and I'm on my way back to Sheshatshiu; the plane has just taken off and I feel nervous but I'm trying to be strong. I wonder why I'm so afraid of flying. If I die, it's only me, not the people I'm trying to help and protect. I should think about them instead of myself. Many of them, including young children, may die in the next few years because of all the problems Innu people have, the destruction of our land and the animals. There's so much illness—heart disease, diabetes—and drugs and alcohol, suicide. We've lost so much!

Nin Tshaukuesh

December 21

Back in Sheshatshiu. This morning after I got dressed, I wanted to go outside, although the weather was very bad, a snowstorm. I went out to feed my dog and then to get some food from the van. Then I made breakfast and went outside again to clear the snow off my tent. There was a lot of it and I didn't have a shovel, so I cleared some of it with my hands but I didn't finish. Nush asked me to come with her to Goose Bay to have dinner with the inmates from Utshimassit and Sheshatshiu in the Correctional Centre.[8]

December 22

Today my grandson was born around seven in the evening, a baby boy, Pineshish's son. He's doing well and everybody is delighted with him. Pineshish wasn't nervous at all and stayed with Munik all through the labour and delivery. I was amazed he stuck it out. I didn't think he'd make it. I thought he might faint. Now he knows what women go through, how hard it is.

Nin Tshaukuesh ·

December 30

I'm always writing my journal. When I'm gone, my journal will still be here. It's an important story, deserving of respect, and I love writing it.

"A statue somebody had made of an Innu woman." Photo of Gerald Squires's statue, *The Spirit of the Beothuk*. Camille Fouillard, used with permission of the Squires family.

Kanani. Photo: Lucas Meilach-Boston.

Tshaukuesh and Francis. Photo: Jennifer and Kerry Saner-Harvey.

2001

January 9

Lately we're really feeling the impact of Francis losing his job at the group home. We didn't have enough food for breakfast today. He was going to cook eggs but there were none left. I was getting ready to go out and he called out to me to stop at Tshak's place on the way home to see if they had any eggs. They didn't have any either, so Francis searched his pockets for change and counted out what he had, not enough, so he asked Matshen if he had some change, a quarter or so, but Matshen didn't, so I searched for change and found a quarter so Francis could go get some eggs. There are no words to express how I feel.

I didn't want to say anything because this hurt so much in my heart, and I knew if I said anything it would just make Francis feel even worse. And myself too. Better to say nothing.

Nin Tshaukuesh

April 10

We started the walk March 4 and finished March 28. When we stopped walking on the last day and put up the tent I felt like crying, both happy and sad, very emotional. Thinking about everything that has happened to the land and the animals, all the destruction, gave me strength to keep going. We finished the walk again and I'm so happy. We made it.

April 11

On Wednesday morning, I went walking on the road at seven in the morning. I was expecting people to join me but nobody did, so I thought maybe they'd be waiting for me on the bridge but nobody was there either. I decided to walk by myself anyway, just a little bit at a time, and see how far I'd get.[9] When I got to the statue of Mary,[10] I stopped to pray for my nephew William Pokue, my sister's son. When I got to Neu Kaitashtet, I saw my brother Shuash Gregoire and he said, "Where is everybody? I thought people were going to walk with you." I said, "I don't know what happened to them. They didn't come." He started walking with me, and after a while we sat down to rest near the lake and Janet Pone came and joined us. She said, "Your sister is in her tent cooking something for you to eat when you get there."[11] When we got to the tent, I went inside to rest and eat. My feet were wet and when I saw my moccasins were full of holes, I realized how far we'd walked. After resting and eating I felt stronger and ready to walk again. My sister Nush joined us too, which made me happy, but we had to slow down because she couldn't walk fast. Shuash and Janet went ahead because they didn't want to walk so slowly. Then Francis showed up with two of my grandchildren, Thea and Megan, and they walked with us too. When we got to Goose Bay we sat down for a bit and took some pictures, then we waited for a ride home. I was very happy. We can do this! I feel very strong now.

Nin Tshaukuesh

April 15

Today we were invited to eat mukushan in Shuash's tent. I didn't want to miss that. It was delicious. Afterward I went to Nishuasht Kaitashtet to take firewood to my tent. I made a fire, and then I lay down for a rest inside the tent and fell asleep. Just a little nap, but Peter dropped by and woke me up again to tell me the news about low-level flying and the military and how they were testing bombs again. He says they're going to expand the test area. I was very shocked when he told me. It's the first I've heard of it.[12]

Nin Tshaukuesh

April 23

Here in Sheshatshiu. Almost nine in the morning. My brother Shuash and his wife came to the house. He said:

I dreamed last night I had a tent right next to your house, and I was trying to get a taxi to take me to Goose Bay to buy some beer. By the time it came, there was a lot of deep snow outside your house, higher than my head, and I tried to convince you that the snow was too deep to go, but you went anyway and the taxi lost control and rolled over and over. Ishkueu cried out, "My

daughter Megan was with my mother in the car!" but just then Megan got out of the taxi, unscathed, and I asked you if you had your seat belts on but you said no. I said, "If you had used the seat belts you'd be hanging upside down in there!"

I thought the dream was a good omen for the protest tomorrow at the base. It made me laugh so much and it's good to laugh.

April 24
Everything went well for the protest. Shuash's dream was a good omen. This is how many people there were:

Me
Nush
Nuisha Penashue
Frances Nui
Katinen Manic and her two daughters
Maninush Michel
Katinen's daughter
Ishkueu Rich
A woman from Quebec, Manitshish
Megan Rich
Nikashantess
Paul Rich
Andrew Penashue
Mishen Rich
Tshak Penashue
Etienne Pasuet

Walkers in nutshimit. Photo: Navarana Igloliorte.

Tshaukuesh and her brother Shuash. Photo: Penashue family collection.

"When I got to the statue of Mary, I stopped to pray . . ." Note four fighter jets in the background, upper right. Photo: Peter Sibbald.

September 11

For a long time now I've been wanting to spend the night outdoors, praying and recording stories about my life and work. Last night my husband went to bingo and I went up the road a little past the statue of Saint Anne to spend the night there.[13] I took a warm coat and boots, sweet grass, a big pot, holy oil, a rifle, and a rosary. When I got there, I made a fire for Innu medicine. I picked ikuta and spruce twigs, boiled them, and strained them to drink. My mother always used to do that so this reminded me of her. I drank it sitting by the fire, saving some for later because I didn't have much water.

At first I was afraid, but after a while I felt braver and then I saw a light behind the hill. I climbed a little higher and stood on a boulder to see what it was. It was a huge bright gibbous moon, and I could feel myself growing stronger and stronger in its light until black clouds appeared in the sky coming toward me from the direction of the Mishta-shipu, and then I felt afraid again. I thought they would cover the moon and leave me in the dark, but they passed over quickly, moving on toward Natuashish and out to sea. The moon lit the sky again.

The firewood was almost gone so I cut more, mixing green and dry so the fire would last longer. Then I put sweet oil around it and prayed, "Please give me courage. Make me brave." I asked the animal spirits to protect me. I told them that even though I had a gun I wouldn't harm them if they didn't harm me. I felt a little braver but not yet ready to see the animals. Things that would seem small in the daytime seem so menacing by night. A barking dog in the distance scared me until I realized what it was.

I phoned my son and asked him to bring me some firewood. I was hoping he'd stay with me but he said, "Okay, I'll come but I'm not going to stay." So I said, "Okay, never mind then." I huddled close to the fire and prayed for a while, and then I remembered something comforting that happened a long time ago when I was a child. My father had sent me to take our neighbours some plates of roasted kaku covered with cloths out of respect for the animal spirits. It was dark and I felt afraid so I sang as I walked through the woods, a song I made up about the moon to keep my spirits up. I did the same thing on the way home. Then my dad said to me, "Why are you so scared? Nobody's hunting you."

I said my rosary by the light of the fire but I started nodding off, so I decided to move around and cut some wood. Then I got out my tape recorder and talked about why I was keeping this vigil, all the problems in Sheshatshiu. There will never be change unless the women all work together. The Innu Nation can't do everything. The women should get together to talk about what we need and how we can help each other. One time the chief told me I should get somebody to take notes at our meetings so we could show the band council what we want.

I talked to the spirits of my parents and all the elders and my sister who died, and I asked them all to help me help my people. Just before dawn I felt very peaceful. I was almost finished my vigil and I felt pretty sure I'd make it. I knew if I did I'd be so happy, and I was looking forward to telling the women all about it when I got home.

About five or so I put all my stuff in my bag and started walking toward Sheshatshiu feeling very strong and happy, so glad I made it through the night. Francis had told me he'd pick me up at seven. I walked a little way along the road and then I saw him coming in his truck. When I got home I was too elated to sleep. Frances Nui and my sister Nush came over and brought me flowers. I told them all about it, and they said next time they wanted to come too. They think we should get all the women together to do it.

Then we heard the news of the terrorist attacks. My son said to me, "What did you pray for last night? God must have misunderstood!"

NEXT PAGES:
Tshaukuesh walking. Photo: Sandra Phinney.

Group photo from 2002 walk: Standing: Tony Penashue, Sylvester Antuan, Janet Gregoire, Frederick Penashue, Angela Rich, Kaputshet Penashue, Tshaukuesh. Seated: Kari Reynolds, Raymond Pastitshi, Lena Napess, Snowdon Piwas, Edwina, Mathieu Penashue.
Photo: Penashue family collection.

Part Four: 2002–2016

Editor's Note

After 2001, Tshaukuesh's diary entries are much more sporadic and most take the form of stories, letters, short essays, and notes on Innu life and events. This was a difficult period. Several of Tshaukuesh's close friends and relations who were also leaders with her in the campaign to protect Innu land got ill and died, among them her fellow protesters Mani-Mae Osmond, Penote Michel, and Tanien Ashini, her sister Nush, and her husband, Francis. Other Innu leaders, including her son Peter, channelled their energy into different kinds of political action, including working on the land claims agreement and its implementation. As part of the agreement process, the Innu held a referendum and voted in favour of the dam at Manitu-utshu. Tshaukuesh continued to speak out against it and was part of protests that led to an agreement in 2016 to mitigate the effects of the dam, by then a fait accompli. Tshaukuesh continues to dedicate her life to protecting the land, water, and all living things in Nitassinan. She has never given up.

The Mines and Dams

So much has happened in the past few years. There are so many things I could say about the flooding of the Mishta-shipu. It didn't only affect the people; the animals are suffering too. Sometimes on our canoe trips the children find small fish dead and they ask what happened to them. At first, I didn't know what happened, why they died. In one of the places where we stop on the river, at the far end of Uinukupau, I was surprised to see a sign on the shore. It said in four languages—English, French, Inuktitut, and Innu-aimun—that we shouldn't take more than one fish per week because of mercury.[1] Why? What are the dams doing to the fish?[2] How many years do we have to live with their suffering? I think a lot about that and about how when I was a child we could eat anything. There was never a sign saying you can't touch this or eat it. There was so much freedom. Now it's not like that. When my husband, Francis, saw the sign about the fish he was very shocked that there's only one sign on the whole river. If they think they need to warn people, why not have signs all along the river? If somebody was camping in a different place they might not know that the fish weren't safe to eat.

I'm concerned about the mine at Emish too. My brother puts nets out there for char and other fish, but soon the water will be polluted. And it's not only the fish that will suffer but also atik\u, kak\u, and pineu. The largest herd of atik\u is in that area. The mine will kill so many animals.[3] The canoe trip is to get public attention to help us protect our rivers. On the Mishta-shipu there are black bears and many other animals. What will happen to them?

There were also important people who used to camp at the site where they want to put the new dam. It's a sacred place, a place where we put the traditional shaking tents.[4] One of the last ones was just above the dam site. It's a spiritual land for the Innu. Before the first dam, Innu people often buried the dead in areas now under water. How many people were born and died there? The government must recognize that people and animals do use the land.

I want to do something about the dam. Nobody is doing anything about it. Why doesn't anybody say anything? I feel as though I'm the only one trying to protect the Mishta-shipu, and I wonder why. If I try to organize a protest, nobody will show up to support me. But I should just do it anyway. I used to just go ahead and do it and it always worked out.

Deaths of Friends and Relations

We used to work together—the Innu Nation, the band council, we all worked together. But the government gave us money for the developments—Emish, Manitu-utshu, so people aren't united anymore, they're distracted and confused by the money. The government paid us off so they could destroy our land. I miss those days when we all worked together. Now the band council seems so busy working for the government that it doesn't have time to work for us. And many of the leaders from the protests have died: Tanien Ashini, Penote Michel, my sisters Maniaten Andrew, Nush, and Mrs. Michel (Penote Michel's mom), Mani Mae Osmond, and Mary Ann Selma.

Other friends died too. When Ann Philomena Penunse, Sebastian's wife, passed away, my sister Nush organized a memorial for her and the women dressed like Mary in blue dresses with veils. Nishapet Pokue (Joseph Pokue's wife), Apenam Michel, and Louis Penashue.

When Nush was dying, I was on the spring walk in Akami-uapishk^u, so I came back and flew to St. John's to see her in hospital. When I got there, her son Christopher was already there. He and his wife were expecting their first baby. He said to Nush, "Be strong, Nika. You're going to live to see your grandchild." But Nush didn't say whether she believed she would live or not. She told me about her dreams. First she dreamed about our mother, and then she dreamed she saw someone canoeing toward her on a lake. We thought she seemed okay and that they'd move her further away from the nursing station since she wouldn't need so much care, so that evening everybody went back to the hotel happy. Only Christopher stayed with her. Then somebody called to say we had to come quickly, so we all went back. I saw Peter in the hallway looking very serious. He said, "She's gone." Her daughters, Janet and Theresa Gregoire, were there crying and Christopher said, "Don't cry. Mom is in Heaven now. She's happy." We knelt down and prayed close to the bed, me and my other sister, An Pinamen Pokue. We asked the Creator to make us strong. Afterward I thought about Nush and all she accomplished in her life. She was a good woman who did good work and tried to help everybody, especially women and children. She was very strong. She always encouraged me and hugged me, and she was always there to listen when I had a problem. She also helped me with writing letters and speaking out publicly. I wondered how I'd cope without her. The next day I went home to wait for the funeral. We were devastated.

My sister Maniaten was always supportive too, and so were her children. I miss those people so much when I protest these days. The last time I went to protest at Manitu-utshu, I had to stay in my tent most of the time because I'd recently had surgery for a detached retina, and I wished my sister could have been there with me. I almost feel I can hear her saying to me, "I wish I could still help you but I'm gone. We never finished what we tried to do." And I tell her, "Let me finish the meshkanau we set out on together." Thinking about that gives me strength to keep going.

Tshaukuesh's great-nephew Mario Gregoire, on a canoe trip near the site of the dam at Manitu-utshu. Photo: Mennonite Central Committee/Nina Linton.

Letter to Premier Danny Williams[5]
June 12, 2008
Dear Mr. Utshimau:

So many years I was going to invite you to canoe trip. Now I want to invite you. Just to know you can see how beautiful the river is, everything so beautiful, trees, river, mountains, long beach, rocks, so beautiful. Sometimes we found a fish dead. I want to know what happened, I don't know. I see a big sign that explain to people not to eat so much fish because of mercury. If you come I can explain more things about the river.

When I was young, when we go with my parents hunting, I never, never forget my dad said before Churchill Falls make a dam, you can see mist from far away. Now I don't see that anymore. What happened? Every time when I go Churchill Falls, sometimes I go with my grandchildren and my husband, always we stop on the beach and I explain to my grandchildren, no water anymore. There was lots of water in paushtuk, the rapids. I am so sad and angry. I am thinking about the fish, and is not only fish, all kinds of small animals that stay on the water. I know animals don't talk, but when I see the animals it hurts me, because the animals drink the water and stay

Sisters, L–R: An Pinamin, Nush, Tshaukuesh. Photo: Penashue family collection.

under the water. We lost so many things that happened because of Churchill Falls—Innu people hunting lost so many things. People used to put stuff on a scaffold, tent and stove and traps and stuff, and they think I come back again, and they all lost under the water. Burial grounds of Innu people who died in the bush, in the country, all under water. This is very sad. I don't know how many men and women and children died in the bush in the country.

When we go canoe trip, I start August 26 for one week. We go to Churchill Falls, take all my stuff, canoes and all, and I start canoeing back to Gull Island and I stop at Gull Island or sometimes Muskrat Falls. Five canoes every summer, last summer six canoes. Innu go, sometimes from Natuashish and Sheshatshiu, and sometimes akenashau, men and women and young children. Start in the morning at ten o'clock or nine-thirty, stop twelve o'clock make fire to eat, sometimes one hour sometimes two hours, and going again. Sometimes weather so nice, very beautiful sunny day, warm. When we have a cup of tea, sit down outside, make some tea outside with big fire, sometimes we cook outside and make a bread on fire. When I get animals like partridge or rabbit, we cook partridge, and we go to the camp in the evening and we eat wabush for supper.

When sat down by the fire, eat, you can see nice rocks, nice clean outside, you can see the sunny day, make me feel good to eat. You want to eat more, it's so beautiful and you happy. I can look, oh so many people, it's getting more people come on canoe trip. I'm more happy when I see partridge, put some snares and next morning get wabush.

If you come with me, it make you more understand why I do things. You can understand me and see me what I'm doing. I can respect to you, I can help you if akenashau don't know nothing. I can help you, where you should sit on canoe, what you should eat, which way we going to go on paushtuk. I can explain and show you.

If you want to come just let me know and I can explain to you more. You can bring your friend or your children and I look after them. I took many, many akenashau on the river and I look after them very good. Maybe if you come, after when you see that river you not going to make another dam. If you come you can see how beautiful river is and the animals. We could have a good talk. I don't get mad, we talk peace, talk nicely, and they ask me questions and I give answer.

Someday, I going to invite you to come to my tent, where lots of akenashau come to see me. If you want to come my tent I make it more nice to show respect to you. Sometimes I'm cooking, sometimes I clean my caribou skin. Queen Elizabeth come to visit my tent—you come too.

I hope you come to visit with me.[6]

Elizabeth Penashue

The Lower Churchill Hearings

March 22, 2011

I spoke at seven in the evening. I didn't get anybody to translate for me. I wanted to try to speak English on my own. I had a photo of my sister Nush in my bag, and Louis Penashue's moccasins. I asked their spirits to help me speak. I spoke for quite a while and I felt as though Nush was behind me, encouraging me. When I finished something happened that I never expected. Peter started to speak, and I was stunned by what he said. He didn't support me.[7] I thought he'd support me, his mother. I couldn't bear to listen anymore, so I walked out and went home by myself. I sat at the table thinking about Nush. She often said, "Don't worry about that," when things went wrong. "Don't worry about what he did." "Make your own meshkanau." "Don't give up, just go forward, Tshaukuesh." Even though she's not here with me anymore, she's here in spirit. I know she can see me and I know she's saying, "Don't cry, Tshaukuesh. You're a very strong woman. Don't give up." After I thought about her I felt better. Nin Tshaukuesh. Nete patshimun.

Uapshish

December 28, 2011

After Christmas, I went camping on Nutapinuant meshkanau with four of my grandchildren: Uapshish, Manteu Iskueu, Manteu, and Mishue. Francis and I put the tent up. I took them sliding and they had a lot of fun. After we

Queen Elizabeth with Tshaukuesh and Nikashantess. Photo: Bert Pomeroy, *The Labradorian*.

"Peter didn't think the queen would go in the tent but as soon as I opened the flap, she came straight in. There were children along the other side of the tent, also in traditional clothing. I told them to be quiet and polite and they were!" L–R: Ani Michel, Mary Madeline Michel, Managanet Rich, Aniet Nuna, Maggie Atuan, Josephine Abraham, with Queen Elizabeth. Photo: Canadian Press/Pool photo.

got home again I put them to sleep on mattresses on the floor. I lay down with them, and then Uapshish wanted to talk about Mishue. She said she felt sad because when their grandfather was ready to go home with the skidoo, she saw me take Mishue's hand and start walking with him and Manteu Iskueu, but she decided to go on the skidoo with her grandfather. Mishue kept looking back at Uapshish as though he wanted her to come with him. While she was telling the story, she was so distressed she could hardly talk but finally she managed to explain how she watched us walking away so slowly because Mishue is so little, and how sad she felt as he turned back toward her, wondering why she wasn't coming with him. I didn't say anything, but I knew how she felt. It was very touching. She's so smart, and so young. Only seven years old. She has such a strong sense of justice—maybe when she's grown up she'll be a lawyer.

Eating Together and Telling Stories

January 2012

Sometimes I'm so busy I don't know where to start. Should I cook, do dishes, wash clothes? I feel overwhelmed. Then I think, at least I'll finish one thing. I try not to lose sight of my goals for the day, but I'm so busy all the time. I have to cook for my family. They don't ask me to but I just do it because they all have demanding jobs. It means a lot to me when they appreciate the food I make for them. Sometimes they invite people over and bring their own children, but somehow, we always have enough food. Sometimes if I've been worried about something, or tired or sad, it goes away when we're all eating together and telling funny stories. That makes me very happy.

Death of a Dog

My dog Blackie died. I know he was old and I had him for many years, but still, I miss him so much. When I realized he was going to die, I kept hoping it wouldn't be in the winter. I'd stroke him and say, "Don't die yet! Wait for summer." One bitterly cold evening I called him to come into the porch but he

Tshaukeush and her grandson Mishue. Photo: Camille Fouillard.

Uapshish. Photo: Melissa Tremblett

couldn't get up. I wished I had someone to help me carry him, but I was on my own so I had to drag him inside. I gave him something to eat and some water. After about half an hour I checked on him again and I saw that he was standing up, apparently feeling better. I called Francis to come see and I was thinking of giving him some of my arthritis medicine, but a couple of days later he went to our old house, where I found him in the basement unable to get up. It was too far for me to drag him home again, so I just kept checking on him every day and taking him food. But one night I slept in the valley in case my daughter-in-law Bernice went into labour, and the next day when I got home he was dead. I blamed myself for going away. I asked Kaputshet to help me put him in a cold place until we could bury him. I was trying to think who could help me bury him under all the snow. I wanted to dig the grave myself and I didn't want it to be too much trouble for Francis so I thought I'd just bury him across the road, but we didn't own the land there so we decided to bury him further away, in the same place where we buried our other little dog. The next day we set out but we couldn't find the spot because of all the snow, so we just chose a place and took turns shovelling snow until we had a bare patch. The next day we went to the valley and borrowed a pickaxe from an Akaneshau to dig a hole in the frozen ground. I took my camera to take a picture and I took my other dog, Ukauiak. After we made the hole, we got Blackie from the truck, but then we realized the hole was too small and we had to dig some more. Finally, we were able to fit him into the hole, though he wasn't straight because he was frozen. Then we wanted to leave, but Ukauiak wouldn't come. He wanted to stay at the grave.

Animal Stories

Otter

Once when I was young and still living in nutshimit, my father got an otter and started to clean it so my mother could cook it, but he noticed that it was very thin, probably no good to eat. My mother said she'd cook it anyway, so he cleaned out all the guts and put them in the water. Innu people don't

Francis and Tshaukuesh at Manitu-utshu before the development began. Tshaukuesh apologizes to the branches she is holding for the future destruction of the site and then throws them into the water. She always thanks the spirits of the water, the plants, and all living things for their gifts. Photo: Penashue family collection.

Tshaukuesh's little dog at the falls. Photo: Penashue family collection.

put the parts they can't use in the garbage or the woods—we put them in the water if the animal came from the water, to show respect. Then my mother cooked the otter meat in a big pot and my father said, "Save the head." Then, after supper, the boys went to bed but the girls stayed up to help my father make a surprise for them. He took the otter head and opened the mouth, then he put all kinds of little odds and ends in it: a small pocket knife, a thimble, a spool of thread, all sorts of things.

In the morning, we all got up and ate delicious crisp fried fish for breakfast. Then my father said, "My sons, I've got something special here for you. Open the otter's mouth, and while you're at it, check in its ears too."

I didn't give away the surprise. I just watched to see what they'd do. My brothers started taking things out of the mouth and exclaiming, "Oh, I found a little knife!" and my father said, "Oh, that's just what I need for hunting!" Then they found the thimble and my mother said, "Just what I needed—thank you!" The boys were so proud of the gifts. When they checked inside the ears they found some tobacco and my parents said, "Thank you so much. We needed this too." And my brother said, "Where did it come from?" My dad said, "I don't know. Maybe otter knew what we needed." My brothers were amazed and one of them asked, "Mom, are you happy?" "Yeah, very happy," she said, "I needed that stuff."

Beaver

For the girls, there was a different story. When they cooked a beaver and shared out all the meat, my mother would say, "Look at how the beaver hands are so small, much smaller than the feet. Girls, you should eat the hands." We asked her why and she explained, "When you grow up, you need to be good with your hands. You want to be skilled at making moccasins and snowshoes, and at sewing. You'll do beautiful handwork when you grow up if you eat the beaver hands." We still thought it was strange so we asked her to explain. "Because beavers work so hard. In the fall when they know it's getting colder, when the frost comes, they work harder than any other animal. They build their house up with rocks and branches and insulate it with mud, nice and warm for winter. Even the little ones help—they bring mud with their little hands and put it on the house. And they cut down all

Ukauiak and Blackie. Photo: Penashue family collection.

the wood they use with their teeth—they don't have any other tools. They all work so hard. Sometimes their hands are so sore they turn from black to white." So that's why my mother got us girls to eat the beaver hands, so we'd be good at all the work we had to do in life. I've never forgotten that lesson.

Another thing about the beavers: the water freezes in winter so they have to stay inside their lodge or swim under the ice to get food. They make an opening in the lodge underwater and in the fall, they stockpile branches and trees near the opening so they can eat the wood until the ice melts in spring. They're very smart animals. They know they have to get heavy wood like birch and aspen so it will sink to the bottom and stay under the ice, and they put it near the opening to their lodge so they can get it easily.

Marten

One time when I was little I was near the tent with my mother, when suddenly she started running in her snowshoes. I didn't know why. All I could hear was a birdcall that sounded like a uishkatshan. I didn't understand why she was running after a uishkatshan, but then I realized that wasn't why she was running. There was a marten in one of her traps. Innu people run when there's a mink or a marten in a trap because they want to get to them before they can escape.

Black Bear

Black bears always stay in their den in the winter—they never go out. When they know the snow is coming, they eat a lot: redberries and blackberries, blueberries. They have to eat enough to get through the winter. They know that if they leave tracks, hunters might see their meshkanau and try to kill them. Somehow they figured out that they have to leave tracks all over the place to hide the path to their den, so they walk in all directions and then jump into the den so hunters won't know which way they went. Occasionally hunters do find their dens, when they're desperately hungry and search for them everywhere, but they're really hard to find. Black bears are extremely intelligent and they know how to confuse hunters, but sometimes Innu will say, "Grandpa, come out, I need food," or maybe, "Grandma, come out," and they do, but they never come out when they're pregnant. It's very rare to find a bear with a cub inside her, but if you do find one, it's a bad omen. It might mean your husband's going to die, or your daughter. Something bad is going to happen. You might find a baby inside a caribou sometimes, but hardly ever inside a bear, and it's only with a bear that it's a bad omen, not with a caribou.

Innu Life

February 3, 2012

A long time ago, Innu life was like a circle, everything was clear to us, but the government brainwashed us. Our lives were whole, we had everything we needed, but now they're fragmented and full of pain. We've lost our knowledge and our strength. In the old days, the Innu were resourceful and knew how to make everything they needed—snowshoes, canoes, toboggans, drums, everything. They were very independent and full of energy. Everyone made a contribution. They respected the land and never destroyed it or took more than they needed, just enough to live, just enough wood for tent poles and to keep the tent warm so the children would be healthy and comfortable. Sometimes they took a little extra if they were sick and they needed the kinds of tree branches they used for medicine, or they'd take some wood to make traps for uapush, mashkᵘ, nitshikᵘ, amishkᵘ, atshakash, or uapishtan. We just cut a few trees, not everything like the Akaneshau do. Who brought these changes? Who destroyed that way of life? We were healthy and happy, generation upon generation. It's impossible to measure all that we've lost. At first, we didn't understand what was happening or what was at stake. I remember that the Innu were afraid of the Akaneshau. And I think the government thought we wouldn't know the difference, that they could do whatever they wanted to erode our way of life. They didn't expect that we would fight back, or that people like my son would be in the government.[8] Now the Innu speak English, they're smart, they're strong. They speak out about their concerns.

Overcoming Addictions

February 10, 2012

Some people go to Brentwood, the treatment centre in Windsor. I'm babysitting my grandchildren while their mom is there. Even though I'm a very busy woman I wanted to do this, because I love my grandchildren so much and I knew how happy they'd be when their mom finished the program. After she left I explained to them that she needed help, that she was sick. Every night I prayed with them. I was afraid she wouldn't make it because I knew how much she missed the children, but she did make it. Sometimes she called me to ask how the kids were doing, and I told her they were fine. When she knew she would finish she called to tell me she wanted one of the children to come to her graduation. Her older son left on February 3 for Windsor and came home on February 5 with his other grandmother. His mother came home the next day and I took the children to meet the plane. They all hugged and kissed each other, and we took her to a restaurant for supper. I hope she'll be strong and not touch any more alcohol. I can already see she's happier and that she understands the difference between before and now. While I was babysitting, sometimes I wanted to do things like go get water on Nutapinuant meshkanau, and I did go but I couldn't walk far on snowshoes because I had the baby with me. It was hard but I managed.

Worries

Christmas 2012

Not too long ago, Francis was quite ill and I was worried about him. He's getting better after seeing the doctor and taking antibiotics. He's still coughing a lot and that keeps me awake sometimes though. I don't want to upset him by telling him that, but sometimes I have to move to another bed. I still worry about upsetting him.

Sometimes I worry there'll be more problems when the new dam starts at Manitu-utshu. I wish I could run away with Manteu and his two friends, and Manteu Iskueu and Uapshish. I think it would be better to take them to live in nutshimit, because then they'd be away from all the drinking and drugs. I wonder if other people feel like this or if it's just me. I know we can never go back to the way things were, but I do wish that the leaders would think about the children and our land and culture. Sometimes my sons and daughters tell me that I worry so much about my grandchildren that I'm going to make myself sick, so I try not to worry and I pray a lot.

The Mishta-shipu

August 26, 2013

I used to go to Nutapinuant meshkanau to get fresh water from a brook there. After they started building the new dam on the Mishta-shipu, I went to get water and saw big trucks and machines and a gate and signs telling me not to come in. I heard we weren't allowed to go there anymore, only workers. Why did they do that? They should let the elders go there and see what's happening, see if the animals and birds are safe. Innu people were there for thousands of years, hunting and using the land and the river. When I was young, people could be confident they'd have good hunting and a happy life with their families. They knew their children would have lots of fresh food to eat. We never saw gas; it was always nice and clean; we could pick berries and not worry that machines had been there and made a mess or left their poisons. When I first saw the signs telling me not to eat the fish because of mercury, I was afraid.

When you're paddling down the Mishta-shipu, sometimes you see strong rapids and sometimes just flat calm water, and when it's calm you feel more relaxed. You're also more reflective, and sometimes we talk about the dam then. "If they flood the river how many metres would the water rise?" I asked, and Francis explained how high it would come. Then I felt so sad thinking about how everything along the shore would be flooded, all the flowers and plants and all the living things. I often think about life before Patshishetshuanau was flooded, and I imagine the people camping along the shore and paddling down the river. How they used to tell their families and their children stories of the past, how beautiful the land was, and how the river would be there for them to live on and to use forever. But now that's not true. I feel that all the work I've done trying to save the land and the river was in vain. I hoped that there would be results, but now I feel that nothing was accomplished.

Mishta-shipu is an important name. The river is alive, just like a human being, and its voice is crying out, "Don't kill me. I'm the water. I don't want to die. Hear my voice. Without water, you cannot live."

Francis's Death

Francis was always healthy and strong, he never had anything wrong with him; he was a good hunter who got fish, caribou, beaver, porcupine, partridge—all kinds of animals for the children to eat. He never stopped: sometimes with Pien or his dad, they'd be out all day getting food for us. The children would be excited, waiting to see what he'd bring. The first time I noticed there was something wrong was when he started lying down for a rest when we were in nutshimit. Doctors used to come to nutshimit to see people, so we asked Jane to come and see him. She said she thought he had diabetes and she gave him medicine and told him to see another doctor in Goose Bay, so he went back to Goose Bay and that doctor confirmed it. That was his first health problem. The next thing was that Kanani and I went camping with the grandchildren, and he had a heart attack while we were gone. Peter came out and told us to come home. By the time we got there they'd already left for the hospital in St. John's, so Kanani, Ishkueu, Frederick, and I flew there to be with him. He had open heart surgery and it went well but he didn't feel up to going on the canoe trip that summer, so two of our children stayed with him and I got someone else to help with the trip. After that, he was okay though, and he always helped with the walks. He was the one who transported equipment, tents, and food for us. After a few years he got sick again. At first, I thought he'd get better, but he couldn't eat or talk very well. Often he'd try to talk to me, but I couldn't understand and that upset him. Once I gave him a pencil and paper and he wrote, "I wish you could understand how I feel." He got progressively worse and they started feeding him with a tube. He couldn't even drink water. At one point, we thought he was getting a bit better, and we were invited to a workshop in Ekuanitshu. We decided to go but then he got worse again and came back to Goose Bay, where they put him on a respirator. Dr. Jong got all of us together—me and all our sons and daughters—and told us he couldn't do anything more for Francis. He said they were going to take him off the respirator. Francis was born in a tent so we wanted him to die in a tent—we all agreed, so we put up a tent outside the hospital and the next evening we moved him there. People came from all over Nitassinan to be with us. He died September 12, 2013. It was very hard. My daughters and

Uapshish and Manteu Iskueu making a toy tent. Photos: Penashue family collection.

186

some of my sons were weeping. We decided to cremate him and take his ashes to nutshimit. We chose Enipeshakimau because that was a place where Francis often hunted, a place that meant a lot to him, where he'd been able to get food and support his family for many years. Some people disagreed with cremating him. It's not the traditional thing to do, but Peter said it was our father, my husband, and that was what we wanted to do. It was very important to me to do it that way so we could take the ashes to nutshimit, and I could see how much it meant to all our children. The weather was terrible—windy and stormy—the day we set out, but we went anyway. One of my daughters-in-law babysat the small children in a cabin, and the rest of us walked up to the top of the mountain. I took tea bags and a kettle because I thought we'd make a fire and have a cup of tea, but in the end it didn't feel right to do that. Nothing was the same anymore. It was always such a pleasure to make a fire and have a cup of tea with Francis, but I just couldn't do it without him. When we were ready to scatter the ashes, Peter told me to go first, so I walked to a beautiful spot and put the ashes there. I spoke to Francis: "I never in my life imagined that I'd be leaving your ashes here in this lovely place where we hunted and fished so often, where so many flowers grow, where we walked together so many times." So many things were going through my mind and I felt I could talk to him about all the things we'd done together there. I told him I'd never forget him, I'd always return to visit him. I looked at the long lake and I said, "Look how beautiful it is, Francis!" The weather was still terrible. We all held hands and prayed in a circle around the ashes, and then the sky opened and there was blue sky right above us. My daughter-in-law saw it from the cabin too. The sky got bluer and bluer and a rainbow appeared. On the way back down, we saw a black bear. I slept that night at Enipeshakimau in my tent with Theresa Andrew[9] and some of my grandchildren, and Nikashantess called me in the night because he heard a wolf. I heard it too and I was scared, but afterward I remembered the rainbow and the black bear. I felt they showed that people were wrong to tell us not to cremate Francis and bring him here. The next spring, I did the walk again, and at the end of the walk when we got to Enipeshakimau we saw a rainbow again, right where we had left Francis's ashes.

November 11, 2013

It's still very hard for me today that Francis is gone. I cry every time I think about the things we used to do, or even when I hear a song or see something that reminds me of him.

My children and grandchildren keep me busy these days. They spend nights at my house most of the time. I try my best to keep myself busy too so I don't get too lonely. I clean around the house and I go out in the woods when it's a beautiful day. Everywhere I go I see all the places where we went together. This month I've been spending my time at my youngest son's house. I woke up one morning and went out and it had snowed the night before. I stepped on fresh snow and I started to cry. I thought if Francis was here he would be walking on fresh snow too.

November 14, 2013

After Francis died I felt very depressed and lonely. I had no idea what I would do or how I would cope. My heart was broken. I was all alone in my house, crying and wondering what I should do. I prayed a lot and a lot of people prayed for my family. It comforted me when all my family was with me, my children, grandchildren, and great-grandchildren. I also felt that doing things the traditional Innu way would help me get through this hard time. I wanted to go walking in the woods, hunting and trapping marten, mink. Then I'd feel stronger. It comforted me to think about my parents, to remember my mother running to her traps when she caught a marten. When Innu people have good hunting, it makes them happy. We don't deal with tragedy the Akaneshau way—with treatment or counselling—but the Innu way—go into the woods, go hunting.

A Broken Promise

January 2014

I'm a woman who has worked for many years to protect the land, the water, and all living things. I think a lot of people know that I respect the animals and the environment, our heritage. I've been wanting to talk about Manitu-utshu for a long time. A lot of people know what happened in the fall, how I lost my husband. This broke my heart, but now my heart is broken again as I look at the river and see Mother Earth suffering, just as I am. Some people are happy about the development, but I'm not happy. When I read the reports and listen to the news, I cry in my heart. I think of the thousands of Innu people who hunted there for millennia. Now the land and water and everything that lived there are destroyed. I really want to go there to see it for myself. It's our land so I should be able to go. We can't know how much damage has been done until we see it for ourselves. When it's finished we will have lost so many things that belong to us, and so many animals and plants will have died. Before Christmas I asked the administration if I could go there to see what's happening, but I'm still waiting for an answer. Are they keeping their promises to the Innu people? Last time I heard from them, they said to wait a while, and I haven't heard from them again. When you make a promise, you should show respect by keeping your word, especially to an elder. They've taken so much from us in the past—our canoes, our tools, our land—but they can't take everything.

Akaneshau Friends

I remember when I was fighting low-level flying, some Akaneshau people heard about it, and they'd hug me when they saw me and tell me how important it was. That gave me courage. Since I began my struggle to protect the land, many Akaneshau want to come to nutshimit with me. I can't even count how many. I always say yes—I'm happy to have them come. I know they'll support me and share my story. I think if they see what we do in nutshimit, what our life is like, and what I do to protect the land, they'll tell others. I never ask for money but sometimes they give me donations. Sometimes they stay in the same tent with us but I worry they might not sleep well because my grandchildren make a lot of noise, so sometimes I offer them a different tent.

The first Akaneshau to join us came on the spring hunt. Then a man from Toronto came, Don Heap.[10] He stayed with us for two weeks and spent the days with me while the Innu men went hunting. I felt safe with him. He never tried to do anything to me, just made notes for a report about our way of life in nutshimit. One morning he saw a pineu, but he didn't tell us because he was afraid we'd kill it. But then my grandson saw it and Francis did kill it and I cooked it for dinner. Francis asked Don if he had seen the pineu, but he said no. Later, at Sunday prayers in Peter's tent, he told us he'd lied about not seeing the pineu, and we all laughed.[11]

Robin McGrath came on the canoe trip and I looked after her. I put her to sleep beside me so she wouldn't be frightened. I first met her husband, John Joy, in St. John's, in his legal robes, when we were in court for the low-level flying protests. I think I first met Robin in Goose Bay, and we became good friends. Sometimes she does sewing for me, patches my pants, and once she repaired my tent after a bear broke into it and tore it—the tear was in the shape of the map of Labrador. Last summer we went berry picking, redberries. She left her car on the road and came in the truck with us. I had some food: fish, salt, butter, bread, tea bags, tea pot, and we got some water from a spring to take with us. After we picked the berries, I made a fire and made tea and cooked the fish. As we ate our picnic I felt so relaxed and happy in that nice clean place, looking at the beautiful scenery. I've been there a few times with Robin; once we went with my two granddaughters, Uapshish and Manteu Iskueu, and Robin said, "Oh, your grandchildren are so young but so strong." Not too many Innu want to come with me because it's a long walk to get to that place. Sometimes I work so hard I don't have time to make supper, and Robin offers to cook for me. Other times I want to ask her to cook, but I'm afraid of bothering her. Even so, she often gives me supper and it's always hot.

Joe Goudie's wife's mother, Lockie Dyson, was another Akaneshau friend. She said to me, "I'm from Mud Lake. I've always hunted and put out my snares, just like you." We were good friends. She came to visit me in my tent on the road, and sometimes I used to see her all by herself, driving along the road with her gun, looking for pineu. When she was sick I went to visit her and she said, "I can't talk very much but I have a Christmas present for you." She gave me a tablecloth and I still have it. I was so sad when her daughter, Joe's wife, phoned to tell me she'd died. I went to her funeral and her daughter said to me, "My mom told me before she died that she wanted to be buried in her nightgown. It must have been her favourite one." I looked in the coffin—she was still a very beautiful woman, and she was wearing the nightgown, as she wanted. I prayed for her. There were a lot of pictures of her on display at the funeral home, including some of her hunting. After the doctor told her she had cancer, she wanted to go hunting one more time

NEXT PAGES:
Francis and Tshaukuesh. Photo: Chris Sampson.

Enipeshakimau. Photo: Lucas Meilach-Boston.

Francis hunting. Photo: Penashue family collection.

so her son took her, and some of the photos were from that last trip. Her husband, Gerald Dyson, died less than a month later, just sat down in a chair and died. He cried and cried at the funeral. Before he died he said he wanted to invite us to supper and his daughter would make us fishburgers, but it never happened because he died so soon afterward. When he died, she phoned me and said, "Someday, Elizabeth, I'll cook you the fishburgers, like my dad wanted." Then she sent me a card to invite us for dinner on her mother's birthday, but I was so busy with my grandchildren that I forgot to go. I felt so badly about it when I saw the card later and remembered!

Another Akaneshau friend from the valley was the bank manager in Goose Bay a long time ago. Once when I'd left Francis because he was drinking, his truck was repossessed, and when I explained that to her she let me put the truck in my name so I could get it back and make the payments. A couple of years ago we were walking on Nutapinuant meshkanau and a truck stopped. It was the former bank manager bringing us some bread. Her husband was with her, and he wanted to meet us because he'd heard so many stories about us.

Sometimes young women from far away want to come to nutshimit with me and learn about my work. That makes me very proud and happy. One was Christina Tellez, the daughter of my friend Jessica, who is a lawyer in Happy Valley-Goose Bay. Christina had a very important dream. She dreamed there were five bears, three up in a tree and two down below. There were people around in tents, and one of the little boys wanted to go play with a bear. We were very frightened because we knew the bear could kill him. The bear opened its jaw and put its mouth around the boy's neck. I looked away because I felt sure this wouldn't end well, but when I looked back the boy was fine, the bear had just licked him. After Christina told me this, I said to her, "The dream means that you should never ever be afraid of Innu people. You help Innu women. If you ever need help yourself, come to us and we'll help you. Don't ever be afraid, just like in your dream."

Another young woman from far away who joined me in nutshimit was Erin Hassinoff, a divinity student from Harvard, who came on my walk in 2001. She came from so far away. I was worried that it would be hard for her to understand what we were doing, but I think she learned from us. When she went back to her country, she wrote about her experiences.[12]

Tshaukuesh making tea in her tent. Photo: Navarana Igloliorte.

Two young women came all the way from France. I can't remember how they got in touch with me, but I think they must have heard about my walk and then they wrote to me or phoned me. Just like when Erin came, I worried about how they'd do. They were so pretty and so young. I wondered, "How are you going to eat our food? Will you be comfortable in our tent? We're going to nutshimit for a couple of months. Will you make it?" I talked to them and explained that I had a small tent for them that I would set up near my tent. I told them that I'd be happy to have them in my tent, but I was afraid it would be too noisy because I had a lot of grandchildren with me. I showed them how to do everything, how to put boughs on the floor, where to put their food and their sleeping bags, and I told them to let me know if they needed anything. My husband took them wood every morning for their stove, and I made sure they knew to close the stove door when they went to sleep and to keep an eye on it always. I explained how to cope without a washroom, and I told them to come visit me anytime they wanted to. They helped me with everything: doing dishes, cleaning caribou skins, playing

Tshaukuesh alone in her tent. Photo: Navarana Igloliorte.

with my grandchildren. After a while I thought, "The girls are going to be okay!" Every Sunday afternoon, if the weather was nice, we went on a picnic somewhere with my grandchildren. Once I was carrying my grandson on my back and one of the girls said she'd take him, but he didn't want to go. I said, "She's a nice girl. She'll just carry you a little way." The girl laughed. And we walked, not too far, until we got to a good place for a picnic.

Sometimes I feel I have more Akaneshau women friends than Innu. I used to have many friends in Sheshatshiu, but everything has changed now and the Innu are divided because of business and money, jealousy. It never used to be like that.

Epilogue

So Many Changes

People used to be very healthy, but now a lot of Innu are sick with diabetes, heart problems, high blood pressure, and cancer. We never had those diseases before. And some people are just tired all the time and don't have any energy because they don't get much fresh food or exercise. We were healthier and happier in the past. But Innu people were very poor then. They had nothing, no blankets, just a caribou skin to sleep on. I'll never forget how when we were small children, we didn't have enough blankets because my mother didn't have the money to buy them. But we never complained.

On cold nights, my dad would get lots of wood and pile it all by the entrance to the tent. He or my mom stayed up all night to keep the fire going, just sleeping for an hour or so at a time. That's why the children never complained about being cold, because they could see what their parents did for them. When we got up in the morning, we never expected bacon and eggs but we usually had some fish or meat and sometimes bread. I loved the way my mother would get it all ready first, and make some hot tea, and then wake us up for breakfast.

In those days, the big girls and boys helped our father and I helped my mom. Sometimes my father went hunting with my brothers, but the girls would usually stay at the tent to learn how to fish or to make moccasins and snowshoes or get spruce boughs for the floor.

Honestly, we never felt as though we had any problems. If you got a cut or had an accident, my mom just got medicine in the woods. And when my dad got a caribou, he used to butcher it outside and put it on a scaffold, because if he left it on the snow dogs or other animals would eat it. One time my brother Shuash and I were playing outside, and I had the idea of doing the same thing as our dad. "We should make a little scaffold," I said. We made one with sticks, and then Shuash said, "Where are we going to get a caribou?" I said, "Try to get a squirrel, kill it and bring it here, then we can cut it up just like the caribou." Shuash went off hunting and I went outside to work on the scaffold, and when he came back he said, "I got one!" We butchered it, the same way our dad butchered caribou. When my mother heard us laughing she asked, "What are you doing?" "We're just playing, just trying to be like Dad." My mother had a good laugh. When Innu kids are in nutshimit they're never bored. They never complain about not having any toys, they always find something to do. They make their own toys and they play outside, and sometimes they have fun imitating their parents the way Shuash and I did.

Francis was my friend when I was young. I had no girls to play with because my sisters were older, so I used to play with him and my brother Shuash. One day they were copying[1] on the lake and it looked like fun. My mother said I couldn't go, but I went anyway and asked them to give me a pole so I could do it too. They gave me a pole and showed me which ice pan to jump to, but they tricked me into trying to jump too far and I fell into the water while they laughed at me.

One winter day, when Francis and I had just started seeing each other, we went to the beach. He was a very good skater and I couldn't skate at all, but he got some skates to lend me and I put them on. He took my hand and kept saying, "Don't fall, hold my hand!" We had so much fun together. We were just kids, just starting to take an interest in each other. He skated backwards and I skated forward toward him.

When I was young, Innu people used to visit each other from tent to tent. People were kind to each other, they shared food, offered tea, told funny stories to make everybody laugh. There was no TV, no electronics, no English. The children didn't ask for money. Everything's changing for the children right now. They're losing their language. Sometimes they try to say something in Innu-aimun but they don't know all the words so they switch to English. Then the parents and grandparents don't understand what the children are talking about. Sometimes I meet Indigenous people from other places, and they tell me they envy us Innu because we still have our language and culture and they've lost theirs. We have to protect it.

Now everything is expensive and the children always want money. A lot of people have vehicles. We never had them before. As soon as one Innu got a car, everybody had to have one. Another thing, everybody wants to go to bingo and play gambling machines. Now people go to bars and this hurts the children. They're sick at heart.

When I was young, I thought the priests worked with God. I didn't understand that, in fact, they worked with the government. They were always writing letters back and forth, and bit by bit they changed our way of life. Nobody realized it at the time. I remember the priest coming to our tent. My mother tidied everything up before he came and he said to her, "It's very nice here. Your daughters must help you a lot." Then he said to my father, "Why don't you go hunting in nutshimit with the men but leave your family here so the children can go to school?" The government and the priests wanted us to stay in one place. They didn't want us to go to nutshimit. After the priest left, I heard my parents arguing about it. My father wanted us all to go to nutshimit, but my mother thought we should respect the priest and do what he said.

I remember one time a big boat came and everybody went out in small boats to welcome it. It was the bishop. Everybody was lined up on the beach, kneeling down on the sand, and the bishop walked along the shore, stopping in front of each person so they could kiss his big gold ring. We respected them so much. Now I would never do that.

So many things we've lost: our river, our animals, our land, our health. I invited an utshimau from Emish to come to my house, and when he came I told him, "One day you'll finish working and you'll go back where you came from. I don't know where you came from: Halifax, Toronto? You'll retire and you'll get a cheque every two weeks, and my people will still be here and our land will be destroyed."

At first, they say they'll give jobs to Innu and many Innu people support them because of that, but it's only at first. Then they say, "Oh, you didn't come on time," or "You got drunk," and they fire them. Then they're unemployed and their land is destroyed. I heard the government say they're going to give jobs to young people so they can change their lives, stop drinking and doing drugs, and buy cars instead and put money in the bank. The government thinks they can help the people by giving them jobs, but it just causes more problems. When they come back to Sheshatshiu they have money and they drink and do drugs. Is that a help? No. I know this because some people were working there. When they came home, nothing. Just alcohol and drugs.

I believe that following the way of life of my parents is showing respect for the natural world. I don't want to be the one who destroys our traditions, a way of life we've followed for thousands of years. I still follow my parents' meshkanau and I'm determined to hold on to their way of life, to their respect for the land, the animals, the people living here now and in the future. We can't give up. We have to keep the earth safe for our children. It's our legacy to them.

Some people still want to protect the land, the rivers, the environment— so many elders have passed away but there are still a few people my age and we have to do something to help the children. Our culture is very very important. Our food, the animals, all kinds of berries, our medicine. Everything. We want to teach the children so they'll know how to live on the land when we're gone. I've told my children and my grandchildren many times: when I'm gone, you have to carry on our way of life and continue speaking our language. School is important, but so is our culture.

"School is important, but so is our culture." L–R: Lena, Uapshish, Quentin, and Mishue. Photo: Tanya Lalo.

May 2017

Sometimes I feel very sad that it's so hard to communicate. I got a computer but nobody has time to show me how to use it. Most of all, I wish my friends could read Innu-aimun. This morning I sent a text in Innu-aimun to Elizabeth. It said, "Hello, my friend. I hope you can understand this. It's me, Tshaukuesh. I wish you could read Innu so I could write you all the time." I was thinking about my friend Frank Gibson too. He can't read or write Innu. But anyway, sometimes when it's quiet in my house, after my grandson goes to school, I sit down and I write my diary in Innu. Here's what I've been thinking about:

I've dedicated my life to protecting the river and the land. I thought it would make a difference. I thought the government would see how much we respect the land and realize that it was ours and they should leave it for us to use. Where are we going to hunt? And our children and grandchildren, all our descendants? When I've gone to join my husband, who will continue this work? We have to teach the children to hunt, to live on the land and look after it.

I want to tell you a story that expresses how I feel:

I'm in nutshimit and I want to walk along the shore of the Mishta-shipu. But everything has changed. There's nowhere to walk—the long sandy beach that used to be there is flooded by the dam. All the trees are submerged and dead; there's gas everywhere and dirty mud where it used to be so clean and beautiful.

And then I see ducks and geese on the water and they call out to me, "Tshaukuesh, what happened? What's going on?" and I start to cry. It's breaking my heart. The birds turn around and take to the air to get away from the destruction and I sit down and keep on weeping. But then I hear them coming back again, and I leap to my feet as they swoop in toward me and land nearby. They're walking toward me, their feet all covered in gas and mud. They say, "Tshaukuesh, don't cry! You're strong. You've always tried to help us. Now we're going to help you." And I feel my courage returning as they fly away, calling, "Good-bye, Grandma!" I watch them grow smaller and disappear in the distance, and then I go back into the woods where thousands upon thousands of trees have died. We only used to take enough wood to warm our tents, but now it's all destroyed.

The beaver used to make a little dam, just a place to live and be safe, but now she has nowhere to go because of the big dam the government made. They need clean water just as much as we do. Almost every morning I pray on the Innu radio station. After I pray, sometimes I talk about Manitu-utshu. They've already started building the dam but we have to do something, at least to show them we don't acquiesce. If we don't, they'll think nobody cares.

These Feet

Sometimes, after a long walk, I take my shoes and socks off to rest my feet. My grandchildren laugh at me. They say I have ugly old feet. But I tell them, "Don't laugh at my feet. These feet have walked a thousand thousand miles."

Still Walking

I was walking by myself one beautiful day. The dogs were behind me and I had my tea and biscuits and I wasn't afraid of anything, not wild animals, nothing. When I got to the marsh I sat down for a rest and a cup of tea, just me and the dogs. The trees were swaying in the wind, all different kinds of trees. It looked as though they were dancing. I wondered why I was all alone, why people didn't want to walk with me when I'm trying to protect the land and the animals, our culture, our children, our way of life. There'll always be money, but if the land is gone, it's gone. I hope people will understand this one day. In the meantime, I'll just keep trying to make a good meshkanau for future generations. I feel as though the dancing trees are my friends, as if they're saying to me, "Don't worry. We're here and we know you care about us. Don't cry in your heart. We're still here, still dancing." It was a clear day and I could see the mountains. Then I put my thermos away again and started walking.

"These feet have walked a thousand thousand miles." Photo: Camille Fouillard.

NEXT PAGE:
"I put my thermos away again and started walking." Photo: Navarana Igloliorte.

Acknowledgements

I want to say thank you to everyone who has helped me with my book. Many people have sent in pictures for my book. Thank you.

I wrote my book with much help from Elizabeth Yeoman. Without the help of Elizabeth Yeoman, this book would not have been possible. I want to say THANK YOU to her and to the many other people who supported this project.

My husband, Francis Penashue, is no longer here to see this book released. My husband was always there for me during our canoe trips, our nutshimit spring walks, and throughout our life, whether good or bad—he was there.

Thank you to my children: Peter Penashue, Max Penashue, Jack Penashue, Gervais Penashue, Bart (Matshen) Penashue, Angela (Ishkueu) Penashue-Rich, Kanani Davis, Frederick Penashue, Robert Penashue, and Francis Robert (Kaputshet) Penashue, and all my grandchildren and great-grandchildren.

I will be very happy once we have completed my book of many journeys.

—Tshaukuesh Elizabeth Penashue (Translated by Kanani Penashue Davis)

. . .

We acknowledge with immense gratitude all the funders, supporters, friends, and relations who made this book possible:

The Social Sciences and Humanities Research Council of Canada (SSHRC), the J.R. Smallwood Foundation, Intangible Cultural Heritage Newfoundland and Labrador, Mamu Tshishkutamashutau—Innu School Board, the Newfoundland and Labrador Arts Council, and Memorial University's Canada Research Chair in Aboriginal Studies all contributed financially to this project.

People who helped translate—both formally, in the early stages of the book's development, and informally, later when Tshaukuesh and I were working together—include Josephine Bacon, Kanani Davis, Laurel Anne Hessler, Marguerite MacKenzie, José Mailhot, Bart (Matshen) Penashue, Francis Penashue, Jack (Tshak) Penashue, Max (Makkes) Penashue, and Angela (Ishkueu) Rich.

Robin McGrath, Jennifer Saner-Harvey, Christina Tellez, and Jessica Tellez, as well as several of Tshaukuesh's children and grandchildren all helped Tshaukuesh write in English so she could send Elizabeth material when they weren't able to be together in person. Robin McGrath also carefully documented media accounts of Tshaukuesh's life and work and—along with her husband, John Joy—made the invaluable contribution of providing a comfortable, quiet place to work and countless delicious hot meals.

Henry Ike Rich, who isn't Innu but who knows Innu land and trails so well, helped with details for the map. Members of the Penashue family also contributed their knowledge of Innu place names and locations, and the Pepamuteiati Nitassinat website (innuplaces.ca) was an extraordinarily helpful resource. Finally, Peter Jackson's beautiful drawings and cartography brought the map and the Innu world it represents to life.

Many photographers contributed to the book. Some of them—mostly family members—are nameless because their photos were a part of Tshaukuesh's huge collection but she couldn't remember precisely who took them. If anyone can help us identify those photographers, please let us know so we can rectify that. Friends and professional photographers whose work we are able to acknowledge are Bob Bartel, Rick Cober-Baumann, Camille Fouillard, Navarana Igloliorte, Jerry Kobalenko, Tanya Lalo, Nina Linton,

Annette Lutterman, Jonathan Mazower, Robin McGrath, Lucas Meilich-Boston, Sander Meurs, Sandra Phinney, Kari Reynolds, Chris Sampson, Kerry and Jennifer Saner-Harvey, Peter Sibbald, and Melissa Tremblett.

One of the most important things about a book is its readers. This is especially true before publication, when their insights help shape and enrich the book. Camille Fouillard and Robin McGrath were there for many conversations about the work, and they also read and commented on drafts as the book evolved. Margot Maddison-MacFadyen also helped with an early draft of the manuscript. The anonymous peer reviewers were enormously helpful, and so were University of Manitoba Press editors Jill McConkey, Chris Trott, and Glenn Bergen, Sales and Marketing Supervisor David Larsen and Copy Editor Maureen Epp. We chose the University of Manitoba Press because they believed in this project and gave us confidence by staying in touch and reminding us of the book's importance over several years as we worked to complete it.

I am also very grateful to Marie Wadden for introducing Tshaukuesh and me to each other, and for sharing her own knowledge and experiences.

I remember Francis Penashue with gratitude and love. I know he had many harsh experiences in the Akaneshau world, and I will never forget his generosity and openness to me, an Akaneshau. His immense wisdom and knowledge of language and the land helped me understand and write about his and Tshaukuesh's world better than I ever could have otherwise.

Thank you also to Francis and Tshaukuesh's family for making me feel welcome in so many ways.

Finally, I thank Tshaukuesh for more than I can ever say in words. Tshinaskumitin!

—Elizabeth Yeoman

Glossary

Aiassimeut – Inuit

Akaneshau – English speaker, European, settler (plural: Akaneshaut)

amishk^u – beaver

atik^u – caribou

atikunanu – a game of tag in which someone pretends to be a caribou and the others try to catch them

atshakash – mink

emikuan mak napatat – potato and spoon race

ikuta – Labrador tea, used as medicine

Innu – human being, First Nation person, Innu. (Note: Innu is a singular form, but it is the form usually used in English. It literally means "human being," but depending on the context is also used to refer to First Nations people in general and to the specific group referred to as Innu in English.)

Innu-aimun – Innu language

Innu-aitun – Innu ways of doing things

Innu-assi – Innu land, Innu territory

Innut kapimutet – Innu walked here.

Innu Nikamu – literally "Innu songs," an Innu music festival

Innu pakasiun – Innu independence and survival

Innutshimau – Innu chief

kak[u] – porcupine

kashustatunanu – hide-and-seek

komatik – Inuit-style sled

kuaskuetshikaunanu – a game like long jump or pole jump

kuatuasikunestkuenest – white-crowned sparrow (its call is "Tante nipatshi nita tshi kutshikutshishin?" "How can I dive down and come back up again?")

mashk[u] – black bear

mashkushiu-nushkuauat – oatmeal (mashkushiu-nushkuanapui is the cooked form, porridge)

meshkanau – path, route, or trail

Mishtikushut – French people, Europeans, settlers

mukushan – a feast held after a successful hunt to honour the caribou spirits

nete patshimun – "That's the story."

Nika – my mother, Mom

nin – me, I am

nin ume nitipatshimun – "That's my story."

nipishapui – tea

nipitekateshimunanu – one-legged or hopping race

Nitassinan – Innu land, "our land"; Innu name for their territory in Quebec and Labrador

nitshik[u] – otter

Nukum – my grandmother, Grandma

nutshimit – This word has many translations, none quite adequate. Translations include "in the bush," "in the country," "in the wilderness," and "on the land." Another translation is "in the interior," as opposed to the sea and shore, but more recently nutshimit is used as the opposite of the community or the reserve. For the Innu, nutshimit can also simply mean "home."

paustik^u – rapids or a portage

pimi – marrow from lower back leg of caribou, a medicine that makes you strong

pineu – ptarmigan, also called partridge in Labrador

pitutshimau – people working for the chief; officials

sikuaskua – wood to hang the pot up over the fire

Tshenut – elders

tshishkuteutapan – train

uapishtan – marten

uapush – rabbit

Uenitshikumishiteu – the powerful creature or spirit living under Manitu-utshu at the Muskrat Falls dam site

Uinipaunnu – Black person, African

uinipek^u – the sea

uishkatshan – grey jay, also called whisky jack in Labrador

uiushun – bundle or load carried on the back

utshimau – chief, boss, leader

utshipitunanu pishanapi – tug-of-war

List of Places

Much of the information here comes from *Pepamuteiati Nitassinat: As We Walk Across Our Land* (http://www.innuplaces.ca) and "Geographical Name Search: Natural Resources Canada" (http://www.nrcan.gc.ca/earth-sciences/geography/place-names/search/9170). However, some places mentioned by Tshaukuesh in her diary are not found at either of these websites, or she gives a different name to the ones found there. In those cases, we have used her names. We have tried to standardize spelling because the Innu Nation has decided to use standardized spelling in formal documents, but in the case of places noted only by Tshaukuesh or where she felt strongly about a different spelling, we followed her spelling suggestions. We also estimated longitude and latitude for places not found at the above resources.

Akami-uapishk[u] – Means "White Mountain Across." English name: Mealy Mountains. Mountain range. Latitude 53.53, longitude –59.04.

An-mani Ushakaikan – English name: Anne-Marie Lake, north of Minai-nipi or Minipi Lake. Lake. Latitude 52.60, longitude –60.87 (estimated).

Atatshi-uinipek[u] – Means "Cut-off Sea." English name: Lake Melville. The Innu name is more accurate because it isn't actually a lake but a tidal extension of Hamilton Inlet on the Labrador coast. Latitude 53.75, longitude –59.40.

Ekuanitshu (QC) – Means "Where Things Run Aground." Other name: Mingan. Reserve. Latitude 64.04, longitude –50.33.

Emish – Means "Amos," referring to Amos Voisey. English name: Voisey's Bay. Known to the Innu historically as Kapukuanipant-kauashat, and to the Inuit as Tasiujatsoak.
Latitude 56.25, longitude –61.90.

Enipeshakimau – Meaning and English name: Pants Lake. Lake and Innu campsite. Standardized Innu spelling is Enakapeshakamau, but Tshaukuesh spells and pronounces it Enipeshakimau. Latitude 53.27, longitude –59.08.

Esker – An esker is a long winding ridge of sand and gravel. The Esker mentioned in the diary is a train stop in western Labrador. Tshaukuesh and her family used to drive there to get the train to Uashat/Sept-Îles before the Trans-Labrador highway was developed. No Innu name. Latitude 53.90, longitude –66.40 (estimated).

Happy Valley-Goose Bay – Town on the Mishta-shipu near where it empties into Atatshi-uinipek[u]. Latitude 53.30, longitude –60.33.

Iatuekupau – Means "Stretches of Willows." Innu campsite.
Latitude 53.06, longitude –58.96.

Innusi (or Innu-assi in standardized spelling) – Currently used to refer to the reserve and surrounding area. However, Tshaukuesh and many elders use it to mean simply Innu territory or Innu land.

Kakatshu-utshishtun – Means "Raven's Nest." English name: Grand Lake. Lake. Latitude 53.68, longitude –60.51.

Kamassekuakamat – Means "Lake in Marshy Area." Lake/marsh crossed on the way to Minai-nipi.
Latitude 52.90, longitude –60.50 (estimated).

Kamikuakamiu-shipu – Means "Red Water River." English name: Red Wine River. Latitude 53.93, longitude –60.99.

Kamit – Means "Across the River" (from Sheshatshiu). English name: North West River. Latitude 53.52, longitude –60.15.

Kanekuanakau-nipi – English name: Sandgirt Lake. Lake and historic Innu campsite, swallowed up by the Smallwood Reservoir. Tshaukuesh was born there. Latitude 53.55, longitude –65.15.

Kapinien-nipi – Meaning and English name: Gabriel Lake. Lake and Innu campsite. Latitude 53.06, longitude –63.35.

Kapitshitinikau Kapakapinisa – Means "The Bombing Range." The area between the Natuakamiu-shipu (Little Mecatina River) and Minai-nipi. Latitude 52.25, longitude –60.90 (estimated).

Manitu-utshu – Means "Evil Creature Mountain." Dwelling place of Uenitshikumishiteu, a large creature like an otter. English name: Muskrat Falls. Site of second hydro dam.
Latitude 53.25, longitude –60.77.

Mashteuiatsh – Means "where there is a point." Reserve.
Latitude 48.34, longitude –72.14.

Matshiteu – Means "At the Point." English name: North West Point. Campsite and meeting place.
Latitude 53.48, Longtitude: –60.04 (estimated).

Minai-nipi – Means "Burbot Lake." English name: Lake Minipi. Lake and Innu campsite, destination of the first walk.
Latitude 52.48, longitude –60.89.

Minai-nipiu-shipu – Means "Burbot River." English name: Minipi River. Latitude 52.86, longitude –61.62.

Mishta-shipu – Means "Big River." English names: Churchill River, Grand River, formerly Hamilton River. Flows from Patshishetshuanau east to Atatshi-uinipek^u. Major river, central to Innu life, culture, and history. Latitude 53.34, longitude –60.17.

Mishtutshashk^u – Means giant muskrat. Lake and Innu campsite.
Latitude 53.17, longitude –59.06.

Natashkuan (QC) – Means "Black Bear Hunting Place." Reserve. Latitude 61.48, longitude –50.08.

Naskapi-shipiss – English name: Naskaupi River. Also known in Innu-aimun as Meshikamau-shipu, but Tshaukuesh calls it Naskapi-shipiss. Latitude 53.78, longitude –60.84.

Natuakamiu-shipu – Means "River Widening Lake River." English name: Little Mecatina River. Latitude 52.11, longitude –60.56.

Natuashish – Means "Small Lake." Reserve.
Latitude 55.91, longitude –61.15.

Net – Meaning of name unknown (perhaps an Innu pronunciation of the English name, Nain). Labrador Inuit community.
Latitude 61.41, longitude –56.32.

Neu Kaitashtet – Meaning and English name: "Four Mile." Campsite on the road from Sheshatshiu to Happy Valley-Goose Bay (Hwy 520). Latitude 53.40, longitude –60.90 (our estimates).

Nipississ – Means "Little Small Lake" (possibly a joke, as the lake is actually quite large). English name: Nipishish Lake.
Latitude 54.20, longitude –60.78.

Nishuasht Kaitashtet – Meaning and English name: "Seven Mile." Campsite on the road from Sheshatshiu to Happy Valley-Goose Bay (Hwy 520). Latitude 53.30 longitude –60.80 (estimated).

Nitassinan – Means "Our Land" and refers to the whole of Innu territory.

Nutapinuant meshkanau – English name: Cartright road. The road from Happy Valley-Goose Bay to Cartright.

Pakua-shipu (QC) – Means "Shallow River." Innu community within the town of St. Augustin, QC. Latitude 58.40, longitude –51.13.

Patshishetshuanau – Means "Clouds of Vapour Rising," because before the dam was built you could see the vapour from a long way away. English name: Churchill Falls. Waterfall and town. Site of first hydro dam. Latitude 53.59, longitude –64.31.

Pekiss – Means "Baikies." English name: Nardini Pond. Also had an older Innu name, Ushtikuan-nipi (Head Pond). Pond at the head of Kakatshu-utshishtun. Latitude 53.73, longitude –60.98.

Pekissiu-shipiss – Means "Baikie's Brook," after the Baikie settler family who had a camp there. Sometimes also known in Innu-aimun as Naskaupi-shipiss (Naskapi Brook). English name: Susan River. Latitude 53.74, longitude –60.99.

Penipuapishku – Means "Rocks Falling Off." English name: Red Wine Mountains. Latitude 53.78, longitude –62.23.

Shapeshkashu – Meaning unknown. English name: Sebaskachu Bay. Bay on Atatshi-uinipek^u, north of Kamit. Latitude 53.75, longitude –60.07.

Shatshit – Means "At the End of the Lake." Refers to part of Kakatshu-utshishtun at its head and also to the Innu campsite on the shore of that area. Latitude 53.75, longitude –60.84.

Shatshit Meshkanau – English name: Grand Lake Road.

Sheshatshiu – Means "A Narrow Place in the River." Reserve. Latitude 53.52, longitude –60.14.

Tshaukuesh Minishtikuss – small island at the north end of An-mani Ushakaikan. Latitude 52.60, longitude –60.88 (estimated).

Tshenuamiu-shipiss – English name: Kenemich River. Flows from Akami-uapishk^u into Atatshi-uinipek^u. Latitude 53.48, longitude –59.83.

Tshenuamiu-shipu – English name: Kenamau River. Flows from south of Akami-uapishk^u into Atatshi-uinipek^u. Latitude 53.48, longitude –59.99.

Tshiashkueish – English name: Gull Island. Innu historic site and campsite. Site of another proposed dam on the Mishta-shipu. Latitude 53.1, longitude –61.26.

Uapush-shipiss – Means "Rabbit Brook." English name Traverspine River. Also known as Manatueu-shipiss, "Little Swearing River," because it's so rocky and difficult to navigate. Small river/brook on the walking route to Minai-nipi. Latitude 53.28, longitude –60.28.

Uashat mak Mani-utenam (QC) – Uashat means "The Bay" and Mani-utenam means "Mary's Town." The two combined form a reserve situated on both sides of the city of Sept-Îles, QC. Latitude 60.04, longitude –53.52.

Uashikanashteu-shipu – This name refers to a story about Innu seeing the bare white feet of an Akanashau lying down on the river bank, and expressing surprise at the unusual sight. English name: Goose River. Latitude 53.35, longitude –60.35.

Uinukupau – Means "Willows Growing at the Mouth of Brooks." No English name, but anglicized spelling of the name, often used on maps, is Winokapau. Lake. However, it is also a stretch of the Mishta-shipu. Latitude 53.16, longitude 62.84.

Unamen-shipu (QC) – Means "Red Ochre River." French name: La Romaine. Latitude 60.40, longitude –53.13.

Utshimassit – Means "Little Boss," referring to a former local Hudson's Bay Company clerk. English name: Davis Inlet. Abandoned Innu village. Latitude 55.89, longitude –60.91.

List of People

Note on Innu Names

According to linguist José Mailhot, "There has never been a time when Innu names were not a puzzle to anyone unacquainted with Innu culture."[1] Compiling a list of people is a challenge for two reasons. First, Innu people often have two or three names: an English or French name, an Innu version of that name pronounced and written according to Innu phonology (for example, Elizabeth is Nishapet), and a nickname in Innu-aimun that is commonly used in the family and community but rarely outside it. Second, in some social contexts it is frowned upon (or perhaps forbidden) to speak someone's name.[2] However, these customs seem to be changing and many younger people use only one English, French, or Innu name. Tshaukuesh herself has gradually become known by her Innu name and has begun to use it publicly. Another challenge with Innu names is that standardized spellings are not always used. The following list uses Innu nicknames or Innu versions of European names for people who are frequently referred to in the diary by those names, along with English versions of their names.

---

[1] Mailhot, *The People of Sheshatshit: In the Land of the Innu*, 71.

[2] I am oversimplifying a very complex system. José Mailhot has a whole chapter on names in *The People of Sheshatshit* that can be consulted for more information ("Personal Names in Transformation," 71–98).

Elizabeth Penashue (Tshaukuesh)
and her husband,
Francis (Katuakueshiss)

**Their children
(partners in brackets)**
    Peter (Manian Penashue)
    Makkes/Max
    Tshak/Jack (Rena Penashue)
    Gervais (Chantelle Penashue)
    Matshen/Bart (Isabelle
    Penashue)
    Ishkueu/Angela (Paul Rich)
    Kanani (Clarence Davis)
    Pipitsheu/Frederick
    Pineshish/Robert (Bernice
    Penashue)
    Kaputshet (a grandson who was
    adopted as a son)

**Grandchildren mentioned in
the diary with parent's name in
brackets (there are also many
more grandchildren and
great-grandchildren)**
    Peter:
    Jean Paul/Napeu
    Ben/Peter Robert
    Thea
    Pupun
    Makkes:
    Tanien
    Tanya
    Kateri

Tshak:
Baby Jack
Cree (adopted by Tshak, son of
Matshen)
Gervais:
Shirley
Elizabeth
Mary Sally
Tshenu/Justin
Matshen/Bart:
Matshiu
Peshinish/Cassandra
Star
Ishkueu/Angela:
Megan
Pishum
Tshimtu/Uniam/William
(adopted by Angela, son of
Matshen)
Kanani:
Nikashantess
Petshish
Matthew
Shaia
Frederick:
Ashley
Pineshish:
Manteu
Manteu Iskueu/Shirley
Uapshish/Roberta
Mishue
Mason
Kanikuen

Tshaukuesh's siblings (partners in brackets)

Manian Asta (Joseph/Shuship Asta)

Maniaten Andrew (Matthew Ben Andrew)

Mani-Mat Ashini (Penote Ashini)

Tashtu/An Pinamin Pokue (Tuminik Pokue)

Shuash/George Gregoire (Shalut Gregoire)

Nush/Rose Gregoire (Richard Adams)

Max Gregoire (Hélène Gregoire)

Fellow activists from the 1980s and '90s
Lists of names in main text:

Shapetesh Abraham

An-Mani Andrew

Ben Andrew

Clem Andrew

Eric Andrew

Kanikuen Andrew

Lyla Andrew

Maniaten Andrew

Paula Andrew

Sylvester Andrew

Penute Antuan

Tanien/Daniel Ashini

Napess/Jean-Pierre Ashini

Selina Ashini

Tshaki Ashini

Shanimen/Germaine Benuen/ Andrew

Ellen Gabriel

Mani-Mat Gabriel

Janet Gregoire

Raphael Gregoire

Judy Hill

Ann Hurley

Mani-Mat/Mary Martha Hurley/Andrew

Natasha Hurley

Pamela Hurley

Bart Jack Sr.

Makan Jack

Penitenimi Jack

Pien Kanikuen

Shanimesh/Germaine Kanikuen

Katinen Manic

Penote/Ben Michel

Manian Michel

Mani-Nush Michel

Shimun/Simon Michel

Emma Milley

Frances Nui

Manishan Nui

Shuashim Nui

Sam Nui

An-Makanet Nuke

Atuan Nuke

David Nuke

Atuan Nuna

Emit Nuna

Jimmy Nuna

Mani-Katinen/Kathleen Nuna

Shuash/Utshesh/George Nuna

David Nuna

Yvonne Nuna

Ishkueu/Mary-May/Mani-Mae
Osmond/Asimin

Mani Pasteen

Mishen Pasteen

Etienne Pasuet

Andrew Penashue

Atuan Penashue

Hak Penashue

Kanikuen/Greg Penashue

Maniaten Penashue

Nuisha/Louisa Penashue

Pinamen Penashue

Shinipest Penashue

Akat Piwas

Nuisha/Louisa Pokue

Rose Marie Pokue

Apenam Pone

Tshanet/Janet Pone/Pun

Anastasia/Natash Qupee

Kari Reynolds

Anne Rich/Nuna

Germaine Rich

Julianna Rich

Kiti/Katie Rich

Mishen Rich

Paul Rich

Tenesh Rich

Mary Ann/Manian Selma

Franceska Snow

Debbie Webb

Notes

Prologue

[1] Dr. Jane McGillivray.

[2] Tshaukuesh's sister Nush (Rose Gregoire) wrote about the role of women in the awakening described by Tshaukuesh: "Because the women have not been involved in these foreign organizations [Innu Nation and band council], it has been almost easier for us, the Innu women, to fight back in this new form of resistance against what is being done to our people. We were never really part of the system that was imposed on us, paid for and controlled by our foreign rulers." Gregoire, "Some People Get the Order of Canada," 240–41.

[4] Author Robin McGrath and Provincial Court Judge John Joy.

Introduction

[1] *Ideas.* "The Least Possible Baggage." Written and presented by Elizabeth Yeoman. Produced by Marie Wadden. CBC Radio, 4 November 2004.

[2] Wadden, *Nitassinan: The Innu Struggle to Reclaim Their Homeland.*

[3] Samson, *A Way of Life That Does Not Exist,* 33.

[4] Higgins, "Innu Rights and Government."

[5] Innu Nation, *Kamamuetimak: Tshentusentimak Nte Steniunu Utat, Nitshish, Kie Nte Nikan: Gathering Voices: Discovering Our Past, Present and Future,* 35.

[6] Innu Nation, *Kamamuetimak—Gathering Voices,* 35.

[7] The Mushuau Innu moved from Utshimassit/Davis Inlet to Natuashish in 2002–3. The move was part of the implementation of the Labrador Innu Comprehensive Healing Strategy, launched following the signing of the 1996 Mushuau Innu Relocation Agreement (MIRA) by the federal and provincial governments and the Mushuau Innu.

8 Sarah Anala told this story at a meeting organized by Memorial University's Aboriginal Resources Office in November 2016.

9 Judge James Igloliorte, *The Queen v. Daniel Ashini et al.* Igloliorte's decision was later overturned because of a technicality, but the Appeal Court did not strike the acquittal from the record and the decision can be used as a precedent in other cases.

10 Judge Robert Phillips, quoted by Catherine Osborne, "Innu Beat Trespassing Charges," 4.

11 Government of Newfoundland and Labrador, "Backgrounder: Agreement with Innu Nation of Labrador," February 26, 2018.

12 The dam is now (2019) being built.

13 Shelagh Rogers, *Sounds Like Canada*, CBC Radio, 14 May 2008.

14 Statistics Canada, "Aboriginal Peoples and Language," 2011.

15 The translators at that stage were Josephine Bacon, Kanani Davis, Laurel Anne Hessler, Marguerite MacKenzie, José Mailhot and Ishkueu (Angela) Rich. They translated notebooks 1–7 (up to November 1995), 10 (spring and summer 1996), and 11 (March–May 1998).

16 Andreotti, Ahenakew, and Cooper, "Epistemological Pluralism: Challenges for Higher Education."

17 McCall, *First Person Plural*, 213.

18 Quoted in Lacasse, *Les Innus et le Territoire*, 249; my translation from the French.

19 Many older Innu, including Tshaukuesh, use the term Innusi to refer to Innu territory, whereas younger people tend to use Nitassinan.

Part One: 1987–1989

1 Quoted in Wadden, *Nitassinan*, 94–95.

2 Ibid., 94.

3 Penashue, "Like the Gates of Heaven," 159.

4 Father Jim Roche was an Oblate missionary based in Sheshatshiu at the time.

5 Bart Jack Sr. was the chief at the time. John Olthuis was the lawyer for the Innu Nation.

6 Tanien is the Innu version of the name Daniel. Daniel Ashini, Tshaukuesh's nephew, was a leader of the anti-NATO protests. He often translated for Tshaukuesh and they frequently spoke together at protests and conferences.

7 Tanien did win and replaced Bart Jack Sr. as chief of the Sheshatshiu band.

8 Chief and band council.

9 Supporters and staff working for the band leaders.

10 The Outpost Program was set up to charter flights so people could go to nutshimit to hunt, trap, and fish for healthy food, to experience temporarily the healthy way of life that was lost when they were moved to Sheshatshiu and Davis Inlet, and to teach the children their culture and skills.

11 Pien Penashue is a highly respected elder and the brother of Tshaukuesh's father-in-law.

12 In 1987 the Canadian Public Health Association Task Force recorded fifteen flights from the base at Goose Bay. One of them measured 128 decibels, almost eight times the noise level of a jack hammer. Cited in *Atlantic Voice of Women Peaceletter*, Dec. 1989, in archived collection of peace activist Betty Peterson's documents at the Public Archives of Nova Scotia.

13 Betty Peterson was a Quaker peace activist from Nova Scotia.

14 In a letter to fellow peace activists Bob and Dorothy Bartel (14 January 1989), Betty Peterson described this meeting:

> Elizabeth Penashue . . . remains my prototype of Innu aspirations and strength. I shall never forget the women's meeting in "our" tent by candlelight, John Olthuis' sensitive and self-searching handling of answers to bold and timid questions was a rare experience, never-to-be-forgotten. There is no such thing as happenstance; I was led to buy batteries for Elizabeth's broken-down tape machine, only to learn later that she taped that women's talk with John, and replayed it over and over again in the silence and flickering firelight in the tent at midnight. I lay there listening; I believe it is impossible to over-emphasize the effect on the psyche of these women for the future. [In archived collection of peace activist Betty Peterson's documents at the Public Archives of Nova Scotia.]

15 Judge Igloliorte's statement is quoted in full by Marie Wadden in *Nitassinan*: "I have no doubt that the strength and determination of the Innu to try and regain self-respect has not been shaken, but rather strengthened in their combined effort to have the authorities pay attention to them. There will be many Elizabeth Penashues that Canadian authorities and administrators are going to have to listen to" (158).

Part Two: 1990–1997

1   Alcantara, "Explaining Aboriginal Treaty Negotiation Outcomes in Canada," 192.

2   Ibid.

3   Government of Newfoundland and Labrador, "Framework Agreement Signed with the Innu Nation of Labrador."

4   Innu Nation and Newfoundland and Labrador Department of Forest Resources and Agrifoods, *Forest Ecosystem Strategy Plan for Forest Management District 19*, iii–iv, 34.

5   Ashini, "Between a Rock and a Hard Place: Aboriginal Communities and Mining," 14.

6   Samson, *A Way of Life That Does Not Exist*, 116.

7   Larry Innes/Es05. . . @orion.yorku.ca, Mailing List: NATIVE-L, 21 November 1995.

8   Canada, Royal Commission on Aboriginal Peoples, *People to People, Nation to Nation*, "A Word from the Commissioners."

9   Kanani Penashue Davis is Tshaukuesh's younger daughter.

10   A komatik is an Inuit sled also used by Innu.

11   This tragedy was a turning point for the people of Utshimassit. Community members conducted a People's Inquiry in which they noted that in the preceding eighteen years they had lost forty-seven people through alcohol-related deaths. The authors of the final report wrote:

> *Our children that were lost in the fire are sending out a message to us for help. We are not listening to our children. We must begin to listen to them. We are gathering voices in this community to help us find the strength to help our children. . . . There were other reasons for this fire too. There was nothing we could do to stop the fire. We have no fire hoses, no fire equipment. Even if we had this equipment, we have no water in the community. If we had water, we might have been able to stop the fire.*

Innu Nation, *Gathering Voices/Mamunitau Staianimuanu*, 1, 4–5.

12   The tour was organized by ACT for Disarmament. Mani-Katinen Nuna, Tshaukuesh, and her son Matshen spoke about low-level flying in Guelph, Hamilton-Burlington, Kitchener, Lindsay, Oakville, Peterborough, and Toronto, participated in meetings at Six Nations Reserve, and led an ACT demonstration in Toronto. *Peace Magazine*, "Notes," 27.

13 Tents have to be moved frequently in spring, because the snow is softening and they become unstable. Moving a tent or setting up camp is an arduous process, as it involves tramping down the snow in a new area to make it even and firm, gathering spruce boughs and laying a new floor, rebuilding the frame and covering it with the heavy canvas tent, setting up the stove and moving all belongings, food, and equipment. However, it is usually done very smoothly with well-coordinated teamwork.

14 Boil-up is the Newfoundland and Labrador word for a picnic with a bonfire to make tea.

15 A march from Mani-utenam to Montreal to protest against hydroelectric projects in Nitassinan. Regroupement de solidarité avec les Autochtones/ Solidarity with Native People Bulletin 14, May 1992. Tshaukuesh flew to Montreal to meet them.

16 It is not uncommon for Innu to travel frequently from place to place in nutshimit and to other parts of Nitassinan (which extends over large sections of Quebec and Labrador). Bush planes or helicopters in and out of nutshimit are often paid for by the Outpost Program (see Part One, n. 10), or people may go by skidoo, boat, or canoe. Travel between towns and cities is usually financed by the individuals or their families unless it is for business or health reasons.

17 There is a shrine at Sainte-Anne de Beaupré where many people believe there are miraculous healings. As well, Saint Anne is an important figure for Tshaukuesh and many Innu, as she is the patron saint of grandmothers.

18 Tshaukuesh was visiting her son Matshen in Ekuanitshu before going to Uashat for the Innu nikamu (literally "Innu songs"), an Innu music festival that also features traditional games, bingo, banquets, and picnics with traditional food, religious ceremonies, and a craft market.

19 The Innu were resuming their campaign against NATO. On October 12, four Innu—Tanien Ashini, Mani-Katinen Nuna, Penote Michel, and Mani-Mat Gabriel—and fifty-one Dutch supporters were arrested at Volkel Air Force Base in the Netherlands, and sixteen Innu women and children were arrested at the base in Goose Bay, though only those over the age of twelve were charged: Janet Gregoire, Ishkueu Penashue, Pamela Hurley, Yvonne Nuna, Rose Marie Pokue, and Debbie Webb, an Inuit supporter. Winkel, "Innu Arrested in New Campaign."

20 The Brentwood Recovery Home is an addictions treatment centre in Windsor, Ontario. It also provides support programs for families. Brentwood, "Recovery Begins Here," undated, http://brentwoodrecovery.com/ecom.asp?.

21 Nine Innu and a supporter from Toronto were sent to prison for fourteen days for refusing to pay fines after occupying Dutch F-18 fighters on 8 September 1993, during a visit from the Dutch Minister of Defence (Survival International, "Innu Imprisoned"). It isn't clear who the rest of the people in jail were and Tshaukuesh doesn't remember, but they were probably supporters who were briefly jailed then released.

22 On October 6, about fifty Innu protesters from Labrador set up camp on Parliament Hill to protest the federal government requirement that they sign the Indian Act. (When Newfoundland and Labrador entered Confederation in 1949, no provision was made for Indigenous peoples and they were not included in the Indian Act.) Utshimassit Chief Katie Rich explained that they believed the Indian Act had destroyed Indigenous peoples, adding, "If we sign the Indian Act, our people will be wiped out." The RCMP informed them that they could not stage a protest or set up camp without a permit. The Innu had a letter of permission from the Algonquin of Barrier Lake, who claimed traditional title to the area, and Innu Nation president Peter Penashue responded, "If you want, you can arrest my people. We are not getting a permit." Johnson, "Innu Protesters Camp on Parliament Hill," 3.

23 The Innu Nation had removed power meters from about eighty houses in Sheshatshiu to protest the fact that there had never been any apology or compensation for their losses due to the flooding from the Patshishetshuanau dam, which provided the power. The provincial government was threatening to cut off power to the houses. Tanien Ashini, then Innu Nation Director of Innu Rights and Environment, responded that the electricity had been stolen from their land in the first place. The government also rejected an Innu proposal for a province-wide energy conservation program in lieu of further hydroelectric development. Smith, "Innu Nation Protest over Power Billing Heating Up," 3.

24 A study of the effect of stress on farm animals raised for meat found that if an animal is stressed prior to slaughter it will produce less lactic acid than normal, resulting in "serious adverse effects on meat quality." See Chambers, Grandin, Heinz, and Srisuvan, *Guidelines for Humane Handling, Transport and Slaughter of Livestock*, 4. In addition, a review of the research on the impact of low-level flying on caribou found that the flights caused a "startle response" that in turn could cause stillbirths, separations of calves from mothers, and injuries, as well as reduced milk production and possibly problems with calf thyroid function, slowed growth, and higher mortality due to stress, weakness, and injury. See Harrington and Veitch, "Short-term Impacts of Low-level Jet Fighter Training on Caribou in Labrador," 325–26.

25 For more information on this protest camp, see Reynolds, "Dead Centre in the War Games," 6.

26 See Part 2 note 18 for a definition of Innu nikamu.

27 Tshaukuesh was going to a peace conference at McGill University.

28 Activist Margaret Cornfoot.

29 The federal government was conducting an environmental assessment in connection with the proposed expansion of the NATO base.

30 In fact, the announcement was finally made in the new year. The Environmental Assessment Panel ruled that there was not enough scientific evidence to support Innu arguments about the harm caused by low-level flying. The flights would continue.

31 Hugh Brody and Nigel Markham, dirs., *Hunters and Bombers* (NFB, 1991).

32 Rick Cober Bauman had worked in Labrador with the Mennonite Central Committee (MCC), which supported the Innu protests against low-level flying. He is currently Executive Director of MCC Canada.

33 The climbers were Johnny Dawes, Jerry Moffatt, and Simon Nadin, representing Survival International. In a press release they stated, "As climbers we have encountered many tribal peoples throughout the world. We would like to support them and to repay some of the help they have given us during our adventures." http://aboutnelson.yuku.com/topic/806#. Wmysw3eZNcA. A video of them climbing to the top of the Nelson Column can be seen at http://www.survivalinternational.org/films/lettheinnulive/downloads.

34 Cloudberries are called bakeapples in Newfoundland and Labrador.

35 Emish—also known to the Innu historically as Kapukuanipant-kauashat, to the Inuit as Tasiujatsoak, and to settlers as Voisey's Bay—was the centre of mining explorations for minerals, especially nickel. The Innu had attempted to evict the mining companies in February 1995 and were still asserting their right to the land. Innu Chief Negotiator Tanien (Daniel) Ashini told a press conference: "Our priority is the resolution of our land rights negotiations and the protection of our way of life. Any potential development in our territory is a major concern." Innu Nation Press Release, cited in Innes, "Staking Claims: Innu Rights and Mining Claims at Voisey's Bay."

36 Net (Nain) is an Inuit community and a base for travel onwards to Emish (Voisey's Bay), where the nickel mining development was ongoing despite land claims by both Innu and Inuit.

37 Tshaukuesh and Peter, along with lawyer John Olthuis and others, were to appear as expert witnesses at the trial of nine supporters of the Innu who had been charged with trespassing, following interfaith prayer vigils at the British and Dutch consulates in Toronto. The vigils related to continued low-level flying in Labrador. The defendants were cleared of all charges, and Judge Robert Phillips concluded, "I hold that the defendants were forced to break the letter of the law in order to prevent a greater evil, that is, to prevent the destruction of the Innu people and their basic human rights." See Osborne, "Innu Beat Trespassing Charges."

38 The discovery of one of the world's largest nickel deposits at Emish and the recent agreement to expand the NATO presence in Goose Bay had brought renewed attention from the media. One of the journalists visiting the camp described the situation in an article for the *New Internationalist*. See Ellwood, "The NI Interview: Elizabeth Penashue."

39 Two Dutch Members of Parliament visited them because of their concerns about the Netherlands' involvement in NATO low-level flying and its impact on the Innu.

40 Melted ice is considered better than snow, because snow gets a burned taste and is often full of spruce needles and debris.

41 Tshaukuesh and Tshak were on a tour of the Netherlands and Belgium during International Action Week for the Innu and the Earth, organized by European peace and environmental activists. The tour included setting up an Innu camp near Volkel, interviews with Dutch and Belgian journalists and CNN, demonstrations at the Belgian and Dutch Ministries of Defence, and meetings with Belgian and Dutch Members of Parliament and Representatives of the European Parliament who supported a fact-finding mission to Nitassinan to look into possible human rights and environmental violations. A key reason for the tour was the recently signed agreement to continue and expand military training activities in Labrador. See Tuinstra, "Innu-Actiekamp Bij Volkel"; and Lackenbauer, "'The War Will Be Won When the Last Low-Level Flying Happens Here in Our Home,'" 147–48.

42 The Innu Nation and the Labrador Inuit Association (now Nunatsiavut) were holding a joint protest at the site of the nickel mine.

Part Three: 1998–2001

1   Tshaukuesh and others had tried to go to nutshimit on foot the year before, soon after Tshaukuesh first had the idea, but they had many problems and didn't make it to their intended destination of Minai-nipi. This year she was planning to try again.

2   When people are in nutshimit, others often visit them, frequently by skidoo but also by bush plane or helicopter if one is available to take them (not uncommon, as it's the only way to travel in nutshimit other than on foot or by skidoo, or on the waterways in summer). It may be paid for by the Outpost Program, or the flight may be going to the area anyway for some other reason.

3   In Labrador, the term "Metis" was used to describe people who were descended from Inuit and European settlers. The former Labrador Metis Nation is now known as NunatuKavut Community Council.

4   Peter had first been elected President of the Innu Nation in 1990 and served until 1997. He was re-elected in 1999 and held the position again until 2004. He was also elected Deputy Grand Chief of the Innu Nation in Sheshatshiu in 2007, stepped down in 2010, and soon after became the Conservative Member of Parliament for Labrador. He was Minister of Intergovernmental Affairs and President of the Queen's Privy Council until his resignation in 2013.

5   The Manitu-utshu (Muskrat Falls) hydro dam on the lower part of the Mishta-shipu (or Lower Churchill) was officially launched in 2010, but planning had been underway for many years before that.

6   This refers to *Spirit of the Beothuk*, a bronze statue of a Beothuk woman by Gerald Squires. In the Innu-aimun original, Tshaukuesh refers to her as an Innu woman. However, "Innu" can be translated as "human being," "First Nations," or "Innu" in the specific sense used in English. In any case, Tshaukuesh clearly has a sense of kinship with the Beothuk woman. We have published a chapter about the statue, the Boyd's Cove site, and translation issues in relation to the Beothuk. See Elizabeth Penashue and Elizabeth Yeoman, "'The Ones That Were Abused': Thinking about the Beothuk through Translation."

7   Probably to launch the book by Nympha Byrne and Camille Fouillard, eds., *It's Like the Legend: Innu Women's Voices*, in which Tshaukuesh had a chapter, as did Manteskueu (Mary Georgette Mistenapeo).

8   Nush worked as a counsellor and did everything she could to help people from the Innu communities who were struggling.

9   This was a walk from Sheshatshiu to Goose Bay, much shorter than the walk in nutshimit but still a substantial walk, about thirty-five kilometres. Tshaukuesh was still using the act of walking as a way of reclaiming Innu land and a healthier way of life, and would invite people to accompany her on these walks as well as on the annual weeks-long nutshimit walk.

10   There are several shrines along the road between Goose Bay and Sheshatshiu, including this one and another to Saint Anne.

11   The Innu have many tents and cabins in the woods along this road. Tshaukuesh usually keeps a tent set up beside her house and another one along this road all year round as well as a cabin near the road. Spending time in these tents and cabins gives a sense of being in nutshimit and a respite from the often-troubled village of Sheshatshiu.

12   The Italian Air Force had just signed an MOU to start low-level flying training at Goose Bay, and there was discussion of new activities such as supersonic flying, helicopter training, winter survival training, and an increased presence of the Royal Canadian Air Force. Economics and Statistics Branch, Department of Finance, Government of Newfoundland and Labrador, "Industry Profile: Low Level Flying."

13   Tshaukuesh keeps a statue of Saint Anne at her house and takes it with her to the bush when she wants to pray, but this one by the road is a shrine put there by Penote Michel's mother, Manian, in the hope that it will prevent accidents when people are cutting wood.

Part Four: 2002–2016

1   A fish consumption advisory from Environment and Climate Change Canada states that lake trout and northern pike from the river should only be eaten once a week. See Environment and Climate Change Canada, "Mercury: Fish Consumption Advisories."

2   In April 2016, the Nunatsiavut (Labrador Inuit territory) Government released a report authored by researchers from Memorial University, the University of Manitoba, Harvard University, and the Nunatsiavut Government. The report examined a number of topics, including climate change and ice monitoring as well as the human health risks of methylmercury exposure from the Manitu-utshu (Muskrat Falls) hydroelectric project. Both Innu and Inuit use fish from the area as an important part of their diet, in a region where store-bought food is extremely

expensive and locally caught meat and fish is generally much healthier as well as more accessible to them. The researchers concluded that there will probably be significant bioaccumulation of methylmercury in the food web after flooding the reservoir. This could be mitigated by clear-cutting the area and removing topsoil. Following demonstrations, hunger strikes, and public pressure in 2016, the province has agreed to ensure that mitigative measures are taken, but it remains to be seen how effectively this will be carried out. For the full report see Durkalec, Sheldon, and Bell, *Lake Melville: Avativut, Kanuittailinnivut (Our Environment Our Health)*.

[3] For a summary of potential environmental damage from the mine at Emish (Voisey's Bay), see Higgins, "The Voisey's Bay Project and the Environment."

[4] For more information on the shaking tent, see Nametau Innu, "Shaking Tent."

[5] The wording in this letter is different from the rest of the diary because it was typed as dictated by Tshaukuesh in English to send to the premier, with only minor editing. Innu words in the letter are not spelled in standardized Innu-aimun (wabush/uapush, paustuk/paustikᵘ, akenashau/Akaneshau).

[6] The Queen had visited Tshaukuesh's tent on 26 June 1997. Premier Williams did not accept her invitation.

[7] Peter Penashue supported the $7.7-billion plan to create another dam on the Mishta-shipu, intended to provide power to the province and beyond via transmission lines and subsea cables. The Innu land claims document, *Tshash Petapen*, promises compensation for flooding from the 1960s Patshishetshuanau (Upper Churchill) dam further up the Mishta-shipu as well as a share of Manitu-utshu (Muskrat Falls) profits. However, groups including representatives of Nunatukavut, Innu elders, the Natural History Society and Sierra Club Atlantic, archeologists, and others expressed concern about the proposed dam. Their worries included the impact on fish and animals, the loss of important historic, cultural and archeological sites, emotional and spiritual connections to the river, loss of navigability by canoe, negative impact on families, culture and communities brought by the influx of money and people, and risk of mercury poisoning because of consumption of contaminated fish and meat (key sources of nutritious and culturally important food in an area where imported food is extremely expensive and often poor quality). For more detail, see Nalcor Energy, Newfoundland and Labrador, Report of the Joint Review Panel, Lower Churchill Hydroelectric Generation Project. There are also safety concerns that part of the riverbank at the dam site may be unstable due to soft, or "quick" clay at the North Spur. See three reports commissioned by Grand Riverkeeper Labrador, Inc.:

Bernander, Lower Churchill River Riverbank Stability Report; Bernander, Safety and Reliability of the Muskrat Falls Dam; and Raphals, Muskrat Falls' Contribution to the Reliability of the Island Interconnected System.

[8] Peter Penashue was MP for Labrador and Federal Minister of Intergovernmental Affairs at the time.

[9] Theresa Andrew is Tshaukuesh's friend and Francis's sister by adoption.

[10] An obituary described Dan (aka Don) Heap's relationship with the Innu: "As Immigration critic, [former NDP MP Dan Heap] pushed for justice. As a pacifist, he opposed U.S. militarism and Canadian participation in the Western war machine, campaigning to end NATO flights over Innu territory in Labrador—a major issue in the 80s. He was part of a group in the party urging Canada to leave NATO. . . . His sad passing has left lots of us out here wishing there were more Heap-ism in our politics and in our everyday affairs. A life of meaning and a shared mission—there's no greater bequest than that." Kirzner, "Dan Heap 1925–2014."

[11] Dan himself wrote about this incident too in his reflections on his time in nutshimit:

> *[Hunting] presented my main culture-shock. City-born-and-bred, I never fired a gun except in the Canadian Army, and then only at paper targets, because the war ended a couple of months after I finished parachute training in 1945. I eat all kinds of meat, and have no moral objection to the killing of animals for food, but for sixty-nine years I never cleaned a fish or fowl because I felt squeamish about killing or handling the killed. Francis one day said to me, "Don, you say you were in the Army and were willing to kill a man, that you're not going to eat. Why are you not willing to kill a goose that you are going to eat?" I had no answer for him. During my stay, I never handled a gun or fish net or rod, nor did I clean a fish or fowl. Two days before I left, I walked past a partridge very near the camp, carelessly scaring it away, and when Francis questioned me I lied, saying I had not seen it. I felt quite ashamed of lying, specially to such generous friends and hosts. . . . Francis was born and grew up on the land, twenty miles from where we camped in so-called "uninhabited" forest and lake country. About 1947, Elizabeth's parents trekked from their summer base near Sept-Iles, through extremely lean winter hunting, all the way to Sheshatshit, more than three hundred kilometres "as the crow flies," taking tiny Elizabeth over the hills on their toboggan. For people of their*

> *culture, killing animals for food is not a sport but a necessity,*
> *and therefore a moral obligation. By my carelessness I showed*
> *my lack of respect for them.* (Heap, Notes on Nitassinan)

12 See McDowell, "Porcupine Lessons: Divinity School Student Spends a Month Trekking with Innu People."

Epilogue

1 "Copying" is the Newfoundland and Labrador word for jumping from one ice pan to another, a traditional but dangerous game for children. It is called "copying" because it is a form of "follow the leader."

Bibliography

Alcantara, Christopher. "Explaining Aboriginal Treaty Negotiation Outcomes in Canada: The Cases of the Inuit and the Innu in Labrador." *Canadian Journal of Political Science/Revue canadienne de science politique* 40, no. 1 (2007): 185–207.

Andreotti, Vanessa, Cash Ahenakew, and Garrick Cooper. "Epistemological Pluralism: Challenges for Higher Education." *AlterNative Journal* 7, no. 1 (2011): 40–50.

Ashini, Daniel. "Between a Rock and a Hard Place: Aboriginal Communities and Mining." Keynote speech, Innu Nation/MiningWatch Canada. Ottawa, ON, September 10–12, 1999.

Atlantic Voice of Women Peaceletter, Dec. 1989. Archived collection of peace activist Betty Peterson's documents, Nova Scotia Archives, Call number MG1, vol 3474 #9.

Bernander, Stig. *Lower Churchill River Riverbank Stability Report.* Grand Riverkeeper, 2015.

——. "Safety and Reliability of the Muskrat Falls Dam, in Light of the Engineering Report of 21 December 2015." Grand Riverkeeper, 2016.

Bouchard, Serge. *Récits de Mathieu Mestokosho, chasseur innu.* Montreal: Éditions du Boréal, 2004.

Brody, Hugh, and Nigel Markham. *Hunters and Bombers.* NFB/ONF, 1991.

Byrne, Nympha, and Camille Fouillard, eds. *It's Like the Legend: Innu Women's Voices.* Toronto: Gynergy Books, 2000.

Canada, Royal Commission on Aboriginal Peoples. *People to People, Nation to Nation: Highlights from the Report of the Royal Commission on Aboriginal Peoples.* Minister of Supply and Services Canada, 1996. http://www.aadnc-aandc.gc.ca/eng/1100100014597/1100100014637.

Chambers, Philip G., Temple Grandin, Gunter Heinz, and Thinnarat Srisuvan. *Guidelines for Humane Handling, Transport and Slaughter of Livestock*. Food and Agriculture Organization of the United Nations, RAP Publication 2001/4.

Durkalec, Agata, Tom Sheldon, and Trevor Bell, eds. *Lake Melville: Avativut, Kanuittailinnivut (Our Environment Our Health)*. Scientific report. Nain, NL: Nunatsiavut Government, 2016. http://bgc. seas.harvard.edu/assets/sciencereport-low1.pdf.

Economics and Statistics Branch, Department of Finance. Government of Newfoundland and Labrador. "Industry Profile: Low Level Flying." *The Economy 2001*. 2001. http://www.budget.gov.nl.ca/budget2001/ economy/lowLevelCont.htm.

Ellwood, Wayne. "The NI Interview: Elizabeth Penashue." *New Internationalist* 281, July 5, 1996.

Environment and Climate Change Canada. "Mercury: Fish Consumption Advisories." 2013. https://www.ec.gc.ca/mercure-mercury/default. asp?lang=En&n=DCBE5083-1.

Government of Newfoundland and Labrador. "Backgrounder: Agreement with Innu Nation of Labrador." February 26, 2018. https://www.gov. nl.ca/lowerchurchillproject/backgrounder_9.htm.

Government of Newfoundland and Labrador. "Framework Agreement Signed with the Innu Nation of Labrador." News Releases, March 29, 1996. http://www.releases.gov.nl.ca/releases/1996/exec/0329n02.htm.

Harrington, Fred H., and Alasdair M. Veitch. "Short-Term Impacts of Low-Level Jet Fighter Training on Caribou in Labrador." *Arctic* 44, no. 4 (December 1991): 325–26.

Heap, Don (Dan). Notes on Nitassinan, April 21, 1995. Unpublished. Elizabeth Penashue, personal collection.

Henriksen, Georg. *Hunters in the Barrens*. St. John's: ISER, 1996.

——. *I Dreamed the Animals—Kaniuekutat: The Life of an Innu Hunter*. New York, Oxford: Berghahn Books, 2009.

Higgins, Jenny. "Innu Rights and Government." Innu Nation, 2008. http://www.innu.ca/index.php?option=com_ content&view=article&id=10&Itemid=7&lang=en.

———. "The Voisey's Bay Project and the Environment." Government of Newfoundland and Labrador, Newfoundland and Labrador Heritage Web Site, 2011. http://www.heritage.nf.ca/articles/economy/voiseys-bay-environment.php.

Igloliorte, James. *The Queen v. Daniel Ashini et al.* Judge's decision, indexed as R.V. Ashini, April 18, 1989. gsdl.ubcic.bc.ca/collect/firstna1/index/assoc/HASH469c.dir/doc.pdf.

Innes, Larry. Mailing List: NATIVE-L 21. November 1995. Archived online at https://groups.google.com/forum/#!topic/muc.lists.indians/wNBicO1jPP0.

Innis, Larry. "Staking Claims: Innu Rights and Mining Claims at Voisey's Bay." *Cultural Survival Quarterly Magazine*, March 2001. http://www.culturalsurvival.org/publications/cultural-survival-quarterly/canada/staking-claims-innu-rights-and-mining-claims-voiseys.

Innu Nation. *Gathering Voices: Finding Strength to Help Our Children/Mamunitau Staianimuanu: Ntuapatetau Tshetshi Uitshiakuts Stuassiminuts.* Foreword by Katie (Kiti) Rich. Edited by Camille Fouillard. Vancouver: Douglas and McIntyre, 1995.

———. *Kamamuetimak: Tshentusentimak Nte Steniunu Utat, Nitshish, Kie Nte Nikan—Gathering Voices: Discovering Our Past, Present and Future.* Innu Nation Community Research Project, Nitassinan, 1993.

Innu Nation and Newfoundland and Labrador, Department of Forest Resources and Agrifoods. *Forest Ecosystem Strategy Plan for Forest Management District 19, Labrador/Nitassinan: 2003–2023.* March 10, 2003. http://www.mae.gov.nl.ca/env_assessment/projects/Y2003/1062/text.pdf.

Innu Nation and Sheshatshiu Innu First Nation. *Pepamuteiati Nitassinat: As We Walk Across Our Land.* 2008. http://www.innuplaces.ca.

Johnson, Doug. "Innu Protesters Camp on Parliament Hill." *Windspeaker* 11, no. 15 (1993): 3.

Kirzner, Ellie. "Dan Heap 1925–2014." *NOW Magazine*, May 1, 2014.

Lacasse, Jean-Paul. *Les Innus et le Territoire: Innu Tipenitamun.* Montreal: Septentrion, 2004.

Lackenbauer, P. Whitney. "'The War Will Be Won When the Last Low-Level Flying Happens Here in Our Home': Innu Opposition to Low-Level Flying in Labrador." In *Blockades or Breakthroughs? Aboriginal People Confront the Canadian State*, edited by Yale Belanger and P. Whitney Lackenbauer, 119–65. Montreal and Kingston: McGill-Queen's University Press, 2014.

Mailhot, José. *The People of Sheshatshit: In the Land of the Innu*. Translated by Axel Harvey. St. John's: ISER Books, 1997.

Mailhot, José, and Marguerite MacKenzie, with Will Oxford. *Aimun Mashinaikan/Innu-English and English-Innu Dictionary*. Sheshatshiu, NL: Mamu Tshishkutamashutau, 2013.

McCall, Sophie. *First Person Plural: Aboriginal Storytelling and the Ethics of Collaborative Authorship*. Vancouver: University of British Columbia Press, 2011.

McDowell, Wendy S. "Porcupine Lessons: Divinity School Student Spends a Month Trekking with Innu People." *Harvard Gazette*, June 7, 2001.

Mudge, Andrew. *Meshkanu: The Long Walk of Elizabeth Penashue*. Black Kettle Films, 2013.

Nalcor Energy, Newfoundland and Labrador. *Report of the Joint Review Panel, Lower Churchill Hydroelectric Generation Project*. CEAA Reference No. 07-05-26178. Department of Environment and Conservation Registration No.: 1305, August 2011. http://www.mae. gov.nl.ca/env_assessment/projects/Y2010/1305/lower_churchill_ panel_report.pdf.

Nametau Innu: Memory and Knowledge of Nitassinan. "Shaking Tent." 2010. http://www.nametauinnu.ca/en/culture/spirituality/ cosmogony/60/136.

Natural Resources Canada. "Querying the Canadian Geographical Names Database." 2017. http://www.nrcan.gc.ca/earth-sciences/geography/ place-names/search/9170.

Osborne, Catherine. "Innu Beat Trespassing Charges." *Windspeaker* 14, no. 1 (1996): 4.

Peace Magazine. "Notes." May/June 1992, 27.

Penashue, Elizabeth. "Life on the Mishta-shipu." *Them Days: Stories of Early Labrador* 37, no. 1 (2013): 122–28.

——. "Nutshimit." *Them Days: Stories of Early Labrador* 34, no. 2 (2010): 45–54.

——. "Miam Ka Auieiat: It's Like a Circle." In *Despite This Loss: Essays on Loss, Memory and Identity in Newfoundland and Labrador*, edited by Ursula Kelly and Elizabeth Yeoman, 246–257. St. John's: ISER Press, 2010.

——. "Like the Gates of Heaven." In *It's Like the Legend: Innu Women's Voices*, edited by Nympha Byrne and Camille Fouillard, 157–75. Toronto: Women's Press, 2000.

——. Diaries, 1987–2016. *Them Days* Archive, Goose Bay, NL.

Penashue, Elizabeth, with Elizabeth Yeoman. "'The Ones That Were Abused': Thinking about the Beothuk through Translation." In *Tracing Ochre: New Perspectives on the Beothuk*, edited by Fiona Polack, 75–93. Toronto: University of Toronto Press, 2018.

Raphals, Philip. *Muskrat Falls' Contribution to the Reliability of the Island Interconnected System*. Grand Riverkeeper, October 2016.

Regroupement de solidarité avec les Autochtones/Solidarity with Native People Bulletin 14, May 1992. Archived online at http://solidarite-avec-les-autochtones.org/sites/solidarite-avec-les-autochtones.org/files/tout%20les%20bulletins%20franco%20résolution%20normal.pdf.

Reynolds, Kari. "Dead Centre in the War Games: Innu Protest the Harmful Effects of Militarization." *Peace Magazine*, November/December 1994, 6.

Rogers, Shelagh. Interview with Peter Penashue and Elizabeth Penashue. *Sounds Like Canada*. CBC Radio, May 14, 2008.

Samson, Colin. *A Way of Life That Does Not Exist: Canada and the Extinguishment of the Innu*. London and New York: Verso, 2003.

Smith, D.B. "Innu Nation Protest over Power Billing Heating Up." *Windspeaker* 11, no. 11 (1993): 3.

Statistics Canada. "Aboriginal Peoples and Language." 2011. http://www12.statcan.gc.ca/nhs-enm/2011/as-sa/99-011-x/99-011-x2011003_1-eng.cfm.

Survival International. "Innu Imprisoned." *New Internationalist* "Update," February 1996. https://newint.org/features/1996/02/05/update.

Tanner, Adrian. *Bringing Home Animals*. 2nd ed. St. John's: ISER, 2014.

Them Days magazine. Archived in Happy-Valley-Goose Bay, Labrador.

Tuinstra, Tuin. "Innu-Actiekamp Bij Volkel," UIT: Ravage #220, October 18, 1996. Archived online at http://www.ravagedigitaal.org/1996/220/Innu-actiekamp_220.htm.

Wadden, Marie. *Nitassinan: The Innu Struggle to Reclaim Their Homeland.* Vancouver and Toronto: Douglas and McIntyre, 1991.

Winkel, Rich, "Innu Arrested in New Campaign." Peacenet, November 1, 1992. Archived online at ratical.org/ratville/AoS/InnuFight.txt.